Dairy Delights

healthy & tasty

DAIRY DELIGHTS
THE HOME CREAMERY

Yogurt, Butter, Cream Cheese, and More

Heidi Huber

h.f.ullmann

Contents

Foreword

Our milk is sometimes respectfully referred to as "white gold." The Bible says that God promised to lead Moses and his people to a land "flowing with milk and honey."

Seventeen years ago I wrote a handy, easy-to-understand book on the subject of dairy processing. At the time, my friend Elisabeth and I were constantly trying out new things and experimenting with small quantities of milk. We wanted to provide our families with a healthy, balanced diet. For us, this included producing our own dairy products that were as natural as possible.

A lot has happened since then. Among other things, I have attended a number of professional courses, and even run a lot of my own courses on the theme of dairy processing, and have learned one thing. You can never know all there is to know about dairy. The wide variety of dairy products available means that there is something to suit every taste. On a separate note, there is renewed appreciation of homemade products. Hosts are once again serving their guests homemade quark spreads, soft cheeses preserved in oil, and fruit yogurts.

Any student of dairy processing will soon discover that knowledge and expertise alone do not guarantee success. Nature itself, through its diverse effects on milk, also plays a part. I am thrilled and excited to be able to satisfy the publisher's desire for a practical book that will generate interest in dairy products in their many forms. My aim in this book is to introduce you to the rich and wonderful world of dairy produce. Simple yogurts and soft cheeses that can be enjoyed immediately provide a gentle introduction to dairy processing. After that, the sky's the limit—let your imagination take flight!

Good luck and happy dairying,

Heidi Huber, spring 2013

Milk throughout history

The origins of dairy processing

I n his Odyssey, Homer describes in simple terms how to make sour milk cheese: "Leave half the white milk to curdle, then place in tightly woven baskets to dry; drink the other half to strengthen you." This is a wonderful description of the essence of dairy processing as milk needs both, on the one hand, our own knowledge of how to produce dairy products, and on the other the influence of natural laws. The production of dairy foods is only possible if we recognize this profound link between humans and nature.

The cradle of dairy processing

People have been using cow's, sheep's, and goat's milk for about 8000 years, although animal husbandry for meat has been practiced for several thousand years longer. Historians agree that dairy farming began in the Near East. Dairy residues have been discovered in the Sahara in ancient clay jars which indicate that the first identifiable attempts at dairy farming took place there as early as 5000 BC. At Saqqara, the ancient burial ground in Egypt, there is a relief depicting a man milking a cow. It is likely that cheese and yogurt were first produced from goat's and sheep's milk. Cow's milk was not processed until later.

Milk consumption guaranteed survival

When humans first began to use milk during the New Stone Age, most people had difficulty digesting it. Humans were not milk-drinkers by nature. Very few people possessed sufficient quantities of the lactase enzyme to be able to digest the milk sugar (lactose). Only babies and infants of up to the age of around 5 had sufficient quantities of lactase at the time.

Over the course of centuries, a gene mutation in Europe and Africa in particular meant adolescents and adults continued to produce lactase and could therefore digest milk and milk products without problems. This development was a crucial factor in survival: the high level of infant mortality was reduced, people lived through years of poor harvests, and fresh milk usually contained fewer bacteria than drinking water supplies. All these advantages gradually resulted in nomads in central and northern Europe settling on one place as crop farmers and stockbreeders. Milk was a reliable foodstuff in places where it was difficult to farm the land, and also in places where it was difficult to preserve food and keep it cool.

From the ancient world to modern times

The ancient Greeks attributed the immortality of their gods to milk. There were even milk sanatoriums in the ancient world, where consumptive patients were treated with milk and whey. The Greeks passed on their knowledge about milk to the Romans, who practiced cheese-making in particular. Cheese became popularized throughout the empire via the Roman garrisons, and a flourishing cheese trade took off. Alongside olives and raisins, cheese was one of the staples of the Roman legionaries.

During the Middle Ages, knowledge about agricultural produce was primarily the preserve of the monasteries. This was where the first books about dairy processing were written, as early as AD 1600—proof of the high value attached to the subject and the need for more in-depth knowledge about it.

Until the 20th century, milk was usually processed directly on the farm. Each farm had its own dairy processing equipment. There was great variety in the products available from one region to the next.

In Alpine regions, for instance, dairy processing was and still is complex and idiosyncratic. To this day, herders and dairy workers, the vast majority of whom were originally male, continue to process the milk into flavorsome cheeses and butter in local dairies. Pastures and dairies at higher altitudes can only be worked in July and August.

In the 19th century, Louis Pasteur (1822–1895) developed the pasteurization process, which prolonged the shelf life of milk and greatly reduced the risk of microbial growth. This laid the foundations for larger-scale dairy processing, resulting in longer transport routes and storage periods.

The emergence of dairies

Until the middle of the 19th century, cows were used mainly as working animals and for meat. The intensive indoor housing of dairy cattle began slowly. The milk was then collected in small local dairies and milk products were produced and stored.

These small local dairies and milk collection points then merged regionally, mostly in the form of cooperatives, so the farmers then became the dairy owners. Dairying developed particularly intensely around 1900, when many well-known dairies were set up. In those days, the farmers would deliver fresh milk every morning and evening, so the dairies also became places where people could meet and exchange information.

The dairy as meeting place

Top: A *Meyers Trinkhalle*, mobile sales stall, in Luetzowplatz, Berlin, in 1928.
Bottom: A milk store in Swabia.

As a child, my father-in-law carried a large pitcher of milk to the village on his way to school using a wooden carrying frame. The milk was then sold to the local dairy and processed. Farmers originally joined together to set up local dairies because of the increased demand for dairy products from a sharply rising population. In addition, because agriculture did not have high material value and many people moved away to work in industry, farms often lacked the labor necessary for dairy processing.

In the 1930s, the German dairy industry was restructured, and all dairy farms were required to deliver their milk to a specific dairy. Cheese- and butter-making on individual farms began to decrease, and with it the variety of flavors. Nowadays, tankers collect milk from dairy farmers or milk depots at least every two days.

Probably the most beautiful dairy store in the world: Pfunds Molkerei in Dresden, which was founded in 1880.

Small and mobile dairies

The trend at the moment is toward large dairies, but small regional dairies are nevertheless experiencing a renaissance. These dairies can specialize in a small number of products, and thus contribute to a far greater diversity in the manufacture and supply of cheese, yogurt, and quark. Their products range from unique sour milk cheeses to yogurts made with fresh ingredients, cheeses wrapped in hay, and cheeses made with herbs. It is worth visiting their farm shops to see the variety and creativity on offer. It is also usually possible to watch the cheese being made and to ask questions about individual products.

There is also a new and very welcome development getting off the ground: the mobile cheese dairy. Although still in its infancy, this nonetheless offers a good opportunity for rural milk businesses to make their own cheese. A cheese-maker comes directly to the farm with a mobile mini cheese dairy and processes the milk into cheese on site. They then transport the freshly made cheese to a designated ripening room. A few weeks later, the finished cheese is delivered back to the farm.

This creates a wonderful variety of different types of cheese, and restores the idea of regional individuality to cheese manufacture. Buying products in farm shops or directly from farmers encourages variety on the domestic cheese market.

The basic
ingredient—milk,
white gold

All about milk production

Milk production is very labor intensive. Milk is enormously dependent on external influences, whether animal health or feed quality. We therefore need to set high standards in our own kitchens when processing milk, and to take into account a whole range of influencing factors.

Milk not only carries bacteria and microbes, it also provides a good feeding ground for them. In general, all farmers pay great attention to ensuring their cows are healthy and that only milk from healthy cows enters the market. The regulations concerning this are very strict and protect consumers, allowing them to enjoy a wholesome, fresh product.

Handling milk safely

Milk production is structured in very different ways. There are still many small-scale farms that only keep a few cows. But the trend is toward large-scale operations, in which milk is produced in large quantities. Milk from cows that graze on alpine pastures has a completely different composition to milk from cows that spend the whole year in stall barns or cowsheds. This has an effect on the products made from the particular milk. Butter made from the milk of cows that are free to graze in a lush meadow is a lot more flavorsome than butter made from the milk of animals that are kept in stalls.

Care, attention, and respectful handling of the animals are all important factors in producing high-quality milk. After all, milk production is an occupation that involves a

Milk straight from
the udder is at body
temperature and
sterile—a special
treat!

strong sense of responsibility. On the one hand, the farmer has a responsibility toward the consumer, whom he wants to provide with a high-quality product, and on the other the farmer has a huge responsibility toward the welfare of the animals entrusted to him.

Milking by hand

I remember quite clearly when I started out as a farmer, before I was used to being close to cows. Before that I had worked in the export department of a confectionery company, and I was very much in awe of cows. Learning to milk by hand was therefore a real challenge for me, and frequently ended with my bowl of fresh milk being kicked over by a cow. I used to be glad if there was enough milk left to make cocoa for our children. The first time I carried a bucketful of white, frothy milk into the house was a wonderful experience.

Nowadays, cows are milked by hand only on small farms and alpine pastures. There is no question that milking by hand is very strenuous. However, once you develop a routine, milking becomes a very satisfying job over time, which also leads to a close bond with the animals.

Modern milking units

Time-consuming milking by hand was eventually replaced by the use of milking machines with collection buckets and buckets that could be strapped to the cows. The development of milking pipelines was a real innovation. They offer the advantage that the milk is transferred directly to a cooling tank via a pipeline and therefore cannot come into contact with the bacteria present in the cowshed.

In modern loose housing stables, cows are milked in milking parlors and automatic milking systems are also common. The use of milking robots has the advantage that the cows can go into the milking parlor voluntarily at any time and be milked automatically.

Larger farms carry out several milkings, which means several cows can be milked at the same time. This saves a lot of time, which can be used to tend and observe the animals.

Top quality guaranteed

Freshly milked milk is a sensitive foodstuff. It is prone to absorbing odorants, and its bacterial content can rise rapidly.

When milk is delivered to a dairy, it is subjected to stringent testing. No other food is inspected as many times as milk. It is monitored very closely. First of all, the milking takes place under extremely hygienic conditions. The milking parlor and the milk tank room have to be tiled. The milk is then filtered immediately, cooled, and collected in a tank. Milk is inherently very susceptible to contaminating microorganisms, the activity of which is significantly reduced by cooling.

Cows receiving medication that could have a detrimental effect on human health are milked separately by farmers and their milk is not supplied to dairies. When milk is collected, the dairy takes automatic samples of the milk and sends them to special laboratories for testing, to determine whether the milk is untainted and whether the animals are sick.

In the dairy itself, the milk is subjected to further meticulous quality testing and then purified. During the purification, the milk is also separated into skim milk and cream. Then, the fat content of the milk is adjusted, again mechanically, for processing and the corresponding amount of cream is mixed in. The milk is also homogenized, by forcing it through small holes at high pressure. This prevents the milk creaming later on, as happens with milk bought straight from the farmer.

The milk that cows produce in the first few weeks after calving is called "beestings." It is not actually delivered to dairies, but instead used to raise calves. Nevertheless, there are beestings supplements available on the health supplements market—for example, in tablet form with concentrated ingredients involving complex manufacturing processes.

It is fascinating
to watch milk
being turned into
wonderful products.

Our milk—highly sensitive product and all-rounder

Milk is a highly sensitivite product when it comes to various influences such as feed quality and animal health but also to all types of bacteria. The composition of milk changes constantly and so products such as yogurt, quark, and cheese do not always taste the same, particularly if you are working with untreated milk.

However, milk's sensitivity is also the property that we can turn to our advantage in dairy processing. Milk can be changed and transformed, simply by heating it up or by adding lactic acid bacteria or rennet. I am fascinated by the wonderful world of dairy processing because it presents a challenge to our intuition combined with our technical knowledge.

No sooner has milk been produced than its composition begins to change. Cooling the milk limits the growth of bacteria, including both good and important lactic acid bacteria as well as undesirable microbes. We can take advantage of the cooling period to collect smaller quantities of milk for processing at a later stage. Heat has very different effects on milk, depending on the temperature. The bacteria in the milk will multiply, but the bacterial growth will vary depending on the culture of lactic acid bacteria that we add.

Valuable proteins

However, milk is not just an all-rounder in terms of its versatility, but also in terms of its nutritional value. For good reason it is the first food given to suckling mammals after birth. After all, it contains all the nutrients necessary for life.

Milk protein contains all the essential amino acids, in other words all the proteins necessary for life. Moreover, the body can use these amino acids to create its own proteins. This is very often not the case with plant proteins, for example, which is why many bodybuilders rely on dairy products.

Fat provides the taste

The fat content of milk is usually easily digestible, and as well as containing fat-soluble vitamins it also transports a range of important flavors. The fat content of cow's milk varies between 3.5% and 4.2% depending on its composition, the time of year, and the animal feed used.

Incidentally, maternal milk contains just 1% fat. This shows how careful we have to be abour fat content if we switch to toddler formula made with cow's milk.

Milk is classified into categories defined by its fat content:

Raw milk fat content	3.5–4.2%
Skim milk	max. 0.5%
Reduced fat milk	1.5–1.8%
Whole milk	min. 3.5%

The fat content of dairy products usually appears on labels as % FiDM (percent of fat in dry matter). This means the liquid part is first removed from a product and then its fat content is measured. Since, for example, soft cheese has a very high whey content compared to hard cheese, the fat content shown on the label as FiDM does not represent the actual fat content. The less liquid contained in a dairy product, the more likely the fat content in the dry matter will equal the actual fat content.

Lactose, the milk sugar

Milk contains around 5% milk sugar, a carbohydrate called lactose. This has become a topic of conversation in recent years as it can cause digestive problems for some people. Lactose intolerant individuals have insufficient levels of lactase, the enzyme that breaks down the lactose and makes the milk digestible. The milk sugar stays in the intestine and can cause pain and discomfort. People with lactose intolerance can control or reduce their symptoms by taking the missing enzyme in tablet form, avoiding dairy products, or using lactose-free dairy products.

Cow's milk allergy is an immune reaction to certain milk proteins. Lactose intolerance, however, is caused by insufficient levels of lactase, which means milk sugar cannot be digested. Cow's milk allergy occurs in babies and infants, and symptoms include allergic reactions such as rashes and itching, but also coughs and sneezes. Lactose intolerance usually appears in early adulthood: symptoms include bloating, diarrhea, and lethargy.

Full of minerals and vitamins

Milk contains many valuable vitamins and minerals, such as the fat-soluble vitamins A, D, E, and K and the water-soluble vitamins C, B1, B2, and B12. It also contains minerals such as calcium and phosphorus, as well as iron, iodine, fluoride, sodium, magnesium, and zinc. Because milk contains high quantities of vitamins and trace elements, it is considered a nutrient-dense food. Milk, sour milk, yogurt, kefir, buttermilk, and cheese are the best sources of calcium.

Ultra-high temperature processing of milk results in the loss of B vitamins in particular, whereas these vitamins are not affected by pasteurization. The other vitamins and minerals are more or less unchanged. The proteins are slightly changed. However, they retain their nutritional value. ESL (extended shelf life) technology has a negligible effect on the nutrients contained in milk. When heating up milk on your own stove, you should always observe the temperatures indicated in order to avoid the unnecessary loss of nutrients.

Sheep's, goat's, and other types of milk

As well as cow's milk, sheep's and goat's milk can be used to make delicious dairy products, as can mare's and donkey's milk, if this is common in your culture. Each type of milk has its own special features.

Sheep's milk

Sheep are very devoted herd animals that follow their shepherd faithfully. Their milk is rich in vitamins.

The production of dairy foods from sheep's milk has a very long history, as sheep were domesticated many years before cows. The Old Testament contains several references that point to a close relationship between humans and sheep. People who raise sheep usually have a close bond with their animals. Sheep are very sensitive and devoted herd animals that follow their shepherd faithfully. Sheep farming with milk production is particularly widespread in southern Europe. The further north you go, the more sheep farming is linked to meat production.

Sheep's milk contains around 7% fat and has a high concentration of vitamins A, B1, B2, and B13, as well as some of vitamins C, D, and E. It also contains important levels of the minerals sodium, potassium, and calcium. The high fat content of sheep's milk intensifies the full-bodied taste of sheep's milk products, which usually have a delicate aroma and a creamy consistency. The wonderful thing about real sheep's cheese is that it melts in the mouth. Nothing tastes better than homemade sheep's cheese crumbled over freshly picked green salad.

Sheep's milk products are frequently used in cosmetics as they make the skin soft and smooth. Sheep's milk soaps are particularly widely available, in a great variety of scents. This milk is rumored to be suitable for people with cow's milk allergy, although this does not generally correspond to scientific facts. Although some people with cow's milk allergy may be able to tolerate sheep's milk, this is not usually the case. Therefore, if you suffer from cow's milk allergy and decide to test this out, you are advised to proceed with caution.

Goat's milk

More than 8000 years ago, people began to use goats as domestic animals, first in the East and then also in the West. These robust and clever animals were later kept by "ordinary people" (craftsmen, servants, and farmers) to produce milk and dairy products for their own personal use. Goats are very devoted animals that require a great deal of care.

Goat's milk and goat's cheese have a sharp, full-bodied taste that is very much affected by the feed. Goat's cheese is often made in small, innovative dairies, which offer a wide variety of goat's cheese products.

Grass-fed milk—natural milk for high-quality cheese

Grassland farming is the original form of dairy farming, as practiced in the Alpine foothills for hundreds of years, and is essential for the production of a particular kind of milk.

Grass-fed milk is the natural raw milk produced by cows that are fed with fresh grass, hay, and grain. This maintains biodiversity in fields and meadows. Cheese produced from pasture milk is particularly flavorful and contains valuable ingredients.

Best feed for the milk cow

Grass-fed milk is not a protected term, rather a self-imposed regulation on the part of the farmer. The quality of raw milk depends on the feed. In a pasture-based system cows are fed green fodder, hay, and a small amount of grain. Farmers who raise cows in pasture-based systems do not use silage or other fermented feed. Allowing the hay to dry naturally, turning it in the field depending on the weather, and harvesting it are all labor-intensive activities. They maintain the valuable ingredients and flavors of the grass. Feed of animal origin and industrial by-products is banned.

Tasty and good for the environment

The properties of the raw milk determine the quality of the products made from it. The taste and consistency of cheese made from grass-fed milk depend on the milk flora. Grass-fed milk contains a range of particularly valuable bacteria, since the consistently non-bloating animal feed has a harmonizing effect on the bacterial flora and helps avoid incomplete digestion. In addition, it contains lower levels of butyric acid, which is not good for cheese-making, and it can be made into cheese straight away without treatment, preservation, or additives. For many cheeses, including Allgäuer Bergkäse and Parmigiano Reggiano, the use of grass-fed milk is compulsory.

Farmers who produce grass-fed milk stand for sustainable land cultivation. They are not allowed to spread sewage sludge or compost on their meadows, and forage areas must not be grazed for three weeks after dung has been spread. The various grasses and plants that flourish as a result provide the milk cows with tasty and nutritious food. As a result, their milk has a particularly delicate, flavorful taste and a high proportion of conjugated linoleic acids and omega-3 fatty acids.

Considerate land management is good for the taste of the milk. Pasture milk farmers go to great pains to use their green spaces in a sustainable way.

How long has grass-fed milk been about?

For centuries, cows were fed with hay in the winter months. It was not until the middle of the last century that dairy farmers began to use green fodder that had been preserved by fermentation. Although feeding with fermented corn or grass does not depend on weather conditions and saves farmers time, undesirable fermentation processes nevertheless cannot be ruled out.

At first, the terms "silo-free," "suitable for hard cheese," and "dairy farm milk" were used to explain the elaborate grass-fed milk industry. The term "100% grass-fed milk" has come into use in recent years.

Goat's milk contains high-quality protein and easily digestible fat (2.7–3.5%), as well as vitamins A, B1, B2, C, D, and E. Minerals such as calcium, potassium, and phosphorus complete the high nutritional value of goat's milk.

Hippocrates and Hildegard von Bingen even ascribed true healing powers to goat's milk, claiming it could invigorate, calm, and soothe. Goat's milk products are meant to be home remedies to treat eczema and promote cell rejuvenation. As far as milk allergies are concerned, the same applies to goat's milk as sheep's milk—it is rarely a suitable alternative for people with cow's milk allergy, despite many recommendations to the contrary.

Dairy products made from goat's milk tend to be popular in sophisticated cuisine since they are more expensive than cow's milk products. Nevertheless, fans of goat's milk can still find a balanced range of tasty products in the supermarket dairy aisle. If you plan to make your own products out of goat's milk, the same basic principles apply as for processing cow's milk. Goat's milk processing is an interesting niche activity for direct sellers.

In small farms, goats are still hand-milked to this day.

Mare's and donkey's milk

Airag (*kumis* in Russian), a lightly fermented dairy product made from mare's milk, is the national drink of Mongolia. The Mongolians have known about the benefits of drinking mare's milk for thousands of years. In the West, however, mare's milk is more often used in cosmetics. Donkey's milk has a similar composition to mare's milk and is also used as a beauty elixir. Cleopatra is famed for having bathed in donkey's milk in order to preserve her beauty.

Mare's milk is very expensive as only a small proportion of the milk ends up being processed or sold. Most of the milk is fed to foals. Mare's milk should be consumed immediately, hence it can usually only be obtained deep frozen. On the southern coast of Sicily, near the city of Agrigento, there is a donkey's milk production plant, the first of its kind in Europe. Otherwise, producers of mare's and donkey's milk are usually small, innovative manufacturers that make niche products and have high standards of quality. As with other types of milk, the suggestion that mare's or donkey's milk is a good substitute for cow's milk in the case of lactose intolerance does not correspond to the facts. These types of milk also contain lactose.

In Russia in particular, the use of mare's milk in therapeutic spa resorts dates back centuries. Mare's milk is thought to have a beneficial effect on liver diseases and gastrointestinal disorders, as well as on eczema, allergies, and acne, and it is also used to strengthen the immune system. Donkey's milk is used mainly in cosmetics. It is believed to possess relaxing and skin rejuvenating properties. Mare's and donkey's milk contain valuable ingredients such as potassium, calcium, vitamin C, and folic acid. They contain significantly less fat than cow's milk (approx. 1.5%) as well as less protein. However, the carbohydrate proportion is higher and both taste sweeter.

Processing milk at home

What is the best type of milk for processing in your own kitchen? Basically you can use any type of milk for my recipes, whether raw or pasteurized. You can even make tasty yogurts and quark using high heat-treated milk such as ESL or UHT milk. For cheese-making, I would use milk as near to its natural state as possible. The more natural the milk used, the better the quality and often the taste of the end product. Nowadays stores offer an extensive range of different types of milk to choose from. Here are a few basic tips to bear in mind when buying milk.

Regionality: If possible, buy regionally produced milk, because the composition of the milk will correspond to whatever grows in the surrounding area. Long-distance transportation damages our environment, so I would advise you to buy regional products where possible.

Organic is without a doubt an important quality criterion for milk, although you should also bear in mind regionality, as mentioned above. The quality criteria for organic milk are very strict and are checked regularly. I would like to see shorter transportation distances being introduced as a criterion for organic milk.

Shelf life: Manufacturing trends are advancing relentlessly toward milk with a longer shelf life. This is of course a great advantage for manufacturers as products can remain on the shelves for longer and transport costs are greatly reduced. There are as yet no long-term studies on the health effects of longer-lasting milk. However criticism is growing, especially with regard to ESL milk. I personally think it is important to read assessments so you can form your own opinion.

Raw milk

Raw milk is a popular choice for making special types of cheese. Climb up to the alpine meadows in the Grossarl valley in Austria, for example, and you will meet many dairy workers who process the milk in its raw state and turn it into delicious products. This is a deeply rooted culture and the milk comes from the cheese-makers' own animals in their own environment. If we buy raw milk from a farm, we need to be aware that we are probably not immune to the bacteria circulating on the farm. You need to be aware of the risk, however unlikely, of the transfer of unwanted bacteria, for example the dreaded *E. coli*. Pregnant women, infants, and people with a weak immune system are particularly warned against consuming raw milk and raw milk products. Therefore you should always think twice before consuming raw milk. In some countries, for example the USA, there are strict regulations governing the use and sale of raw milk to consumers on hygiene grounds.

If you decide to use raw milk at your own risk, you should always heat it before use according to specific rules. However, for the recipes in this book I strongly recommend using only pasteurized milk.

Processing treated milk

If you are working with fresh milk that has been pasteurized and homogenized, the milk has already been processed. It is therefore usually free of unwanted bacteria, but will still contain a sufficient amount of bacteria that are common in milk. From a taste point of view, these products do not quite match up to those made from raw milk, but they nevertheless achieve outstanding quality.

In principle you can also use ESL and UHT milk. However, UHT milk products in particular can produce a taste of boiled milk. If you want to make cheese, it is better not to use UHT milk. Ultra-high temperature processing (1–4 seconds at above 275 °F / 135 °C) kills nearly all bacteria, including the "good" ones. You can even make a variety of dairy products from lactose-free milk. Nevertheless, dairy products in which the lactose has been broken down by lactic acid bacteria (yogurt, kefir, sour milk products), or from which the lactose has been removed with the whey (soft and hard cheese), no longer contain large quantities of lactose anyway, and are easier to digest.

Finally: always work in a clean environment

Milk will not tolerate the smallest amount of dirt—hygiene is the cardinal rule! It is therefore a good idea to check where sources of harmful bacteria growth might be. The sink unit, for example, is a place where unwanted bacteria can easily grow. Cleaning cloths and sponges should be washed every day, otherwise they are real breeding grounds for bacteria. The refrigerator should also be cleaned regularly.

If you make dairy products in your own home, you should use your own equipment such as pans, whisks, and knives. These should be washed regularly in boiling water, and then rinsed in cold water. This also applies to sink units, which should be given a final rinse with cold water each time they are cleaned, as a warm environment encourages the growth of unwanted bacteria.

Using a special food thermometer, you can heat milk to the required temperature.

Yogurt— health from the kitchen

On everyone's lips

Nowadays, yogurt is probably the most popular dairy product of all, and one of the most versatile. And it is quite simple to make it at home. I always think it is like watching a little miracle, the way milk turns into yogurt a few hours after adding lactic acid bacteria. There are then plenty of ways to use it—in deliciously refreshing yogurt drinks, spicy dressings, and yummy cakes.

Culinary chameleon

Homemade yogurt is a high-quality food, provided you use milk that is as fresh as possible. Once the yogurt is ready, it is a matter of deciding which additional ingredients to add to it, whether it is homemade jam, freshly picked wild herbs, or edible flowers. For sweetening, stevia (a natural sugar substitute) and honey are both good options.

Yogurt is a healthy and easily digestible foodstuff. It is useful for making dressings and sauces, especially if you want a "lite" or low-calorie alternative to richer cream or butter-based sauces.

If yogurt is kept in the fridge, it should always be in a sealed container, like all dairy products. This is because milk and dairy products absorb nearly all foreign odors very readily. If you do not have the time to make your own yogurt, you can buy some readymade and use my recipes to create yogurt in a wide variety of flavors.

Yogurt from all over the world

When I was young, there were two types of yogurt: "natural" and "strawberry." Nowadays when you stand in front of the chiller section of a food store, the array of yogurts is almost overwhelming, from natural yogurt containing just milk or cream and yogurt cultures through coffee and vanilla yogurt, and not forgetting strawberry, cherry, and passion fruit flavors.

In the Anglo-Saxon world, products such as yogurt shakes and frozen yogurt—a light, chilled dessert that comes in many varieties—are also very popular. Ayran, lassi, and kefir are consumed widely in the Middle and Far East. And, last but not least, the Scandinavian countries nearly all have their own yogurt variations—whether it is ymer from Denmark, filmjölk from Sweden, or viili from Finland.

Significant health benefits

Knowledge passed down over the years has consistently pointed out the significant health benefits of yogurt. People are advised to eat yogurt after taking antibiotics, for example, in order to stabilize the intestinal flora. Yogurt can stimulate the digestion and have a positive effect on bone structure.

Then there are those types of yogurts that, according to the adverts, are particularly good for intestinal health. These are very expensive and are heavily advertised. After all, who does not want to improve their health? The message about clockwise-rotating active lactic acid bacteria that have an effect on the intestinal flora sounds plausible and self-evident. There are studies that prove their effect. Others, on the other hand, are more cautious.

The fact is that the "normal" lactic acid bacteria cultures in natural yogurt also act as a necessary regulator in the intestine, restraining negative or harmful bacteria. Probiotic dairy products contain bacteria cultures that resemble the lactic acid bacteria present in the human intestine. Prebiotics, on the other hand, are not usually dairy products, but products that just help the body increase its amount of beneficial lactic acid bacteria.

Rich in nutrients

Yogurt contains lots of valuable calcium, which can be put to good use by the body. Vitamins A, B2, and B12 are also abundant in yogurt, and minerals such as potassium, phosphorus, and magnesium are present in significant amounts.

Yogurt contains between 0.1% and 10% fat. A very low fat content is usually at the expense of taste. Yogurt with a 10% fat content has a much more intense taste, because fat is a natural flavor enhancer. Moreover, products with a higher fat content keep you feeling full for longer.

Standard yogurt contains 3.5 to 3.8% fat, while low fat varieties contain 1.5 to 1.8% fat. There is also yogurt made from skim milk, which has a maximum 0.5% fat. Cream yogurt contains at least 10% fat.

Yogurt contains an average of 3% protein and 4% carbohydrate, the latter mainly in the form of lactose. The protein in yogurt can be easily digested and used by the body.

Yogurt contains all the important ingredients found in milk. If it is low in fat, it will contain fewer fat-soluble vitamins.

Beauty aid

Yogurt has also long been used as a home remedy for skincare. The milk sugar or lactose it contains is thought to lock moisture into the cells. After treatment with yogurt, the skin looks fresher and tauter.

To make a **simple face mask**, mix together 2 tablespoons of natural yogurt (3.5% fat) with 1 tablespoon of honey and 2 tablespoons of oat flakes and apply this mixture to the skin, avoiding the eyes. Allow the mask to work on the skin for 10 minutes and then wash off completely with warm water.

All about yogurt-making

Yogurt naturally has a slightly sour taste and therefore goes well with sweet fruit such as grapes. Or you can sweeten it with crunchy cookies.

Yogurt is made from milk through the fermentation of lactic acid. If you add lactic acid bacteria to milk, the bacteria will convert the lactose into lactic acid, and the milk protein will curdle. Once the protein has curdled, the yogurt will no longer be liquid like milk, but viscous or jellylike. What is more, the lactic acid thus created will lengthen the shelf life of the yogurt, like a type of natural preservative.

The typical yogurt cultures *lactobacillus bulgaricus* and *streptococcus thermophilus*, which can be added to milk or cream, are essential. Both bacteria thrive at relatively high temperatures (= thermophilic), which is why the temperatures required for making yogurt are higher than those required for making sour milk products.

Milk, a valuable starting product

You can use all types of milk to make yogurt. Milk naturally contains different amounts of lactic acid bacteria depending on how it has been processed. Raw milk, which has not been cooled or processed in any way, contains the highest proportion of its own active lactic acid bacteria (but possibly also microbes or bacteria). After that come heat-treated fresh milk and fresh organic milk. UHT milk contains the fewest lactic acid bacteria. Incidentally, milk straight from the udder is still sterile. It is only when it comes into contact with the air that it is beset by various bacteria.

The correct temperature

Thermophilic lactic acid cultures for yogurt require a temperature of 108–113 °F (42–45 °C). You should keep the temperature as precise as possible as it has a huge influence on the multiplication of the lactic acid bacteria.

The milk is heated while stirring constantly. When the milk has nearly reached the desired temperature, remove the pan from the stove. Milk that is being prepared in a pan with a regular base will continue to heat up by about 3.6 °F (2 °C). On the other hand, milk in a pan with a thermal base will continue to heat up by up to 10 °F (6 °C). You should therefore avoid using pans with thermal bases to make yogurt.

A thermometer is important for making yogurt, as the temperature of the milk into which the lactic acid culture is stirred needs to be maintained very precisely. You can buy special food thermometers for dairy processing from a supplier of precision temperature instruments or a specialized dairy goods supplier.

I prefer a simple food thermometer about 12 in (30 cm) long, which is easy to dip into the milk. If you are processing larger quantities of milk, I would recommend using a thermometer with a wire or wooden casing as you can suspend this in the milk. For standard home use, however, an easy-to-clean food thermometer without casing is sufficient.

Inoculating with yogurt cultures

A quick addition of the right lactic acid bacteria stems the growth of unwanted bacteria and microbes, and initiates the multiplication of the yogurt cultures and thus the formation of yogurt. One method of making yogurt involves buying prepared yogurt cultures. Alternatively, you can use readymade, commercially available natural yogurt which is also a good way of adding lactic acid bacteria to the milk.

Clockwise- and anticlockwise-rotating lactic acids

You may already have heard of clockwise L (+)- and anticlockwise D (–)- rotating lactic acid. The difference is according to whether the lactic acid rotates linearly polarized light to the right or the left under laboratory conditions. However, there is insufficient scientific proof of the health benefits of either one or the other, and according to current knowledge both variants are equally good for health.

Mild or sour, semisolid or creamy?

By adding the relevant yogurt cultures, you can also decide whether you would prefer your yogurt slightly sour or milder. If you buy readymade cultures, the packaging will state what kind of yogurt the culture will make. Traditionally yogurt was made with *lactobacillus bulgaricus*, which produces a relatively sour taste. In order to obtain a milder yogurt, dairy technologists replaced *lactobacillus bulgaricus* with *lactobacillus acidophilus* and *bifidobacterium bifido*. Always check the label to find out whether a yogurt has been made using "mild-flavor" cultures.

You can usually find both mild and standard yogurt in semisolid and stirred or drinkable form (drinking yogurt). Semisolid products mature directly in the yogurt cup or jar. Stirred yogurt, on the other hand, is first incubated in tanks and then filled afterward. Drinking yogurt is homogenized after it has been made, in order to return the gelatinous mass to a liquid state.

Yogurt maker

There are two main types of yogurt maker on the market, one with individual screw lid jars (usually 6 jars) and one with a container of 4 cups (1 liter) capacity. Which version you choose will depend on how you intend to use the yogurt afterward. If you plan to enjoy the yogurt "naturally" or just to add some jam, jars with screw lids are ideal. If you use yogurt regularly in the kitchen for dressings, yogurt drinks, muesli, or baking, a yogurt maker with a single large container is more suitable.

A yogurt maker is relatively cheap and helps to maintain the correct temperature.

It is worthwhile buying additional jars, so you can make more yogurt while there are still jars in the fridge. Simple machines without additional functionality are perfectly adequate (see the appendix on page 160). If you plan to make yogurt, I would definitely recommend using a yogurt maker. This guarantees a steady temperature, which means the lactic acid bacteria can grow as they should.

What are sour milk products?

Even though yogurt is generally assumed to be a sour milk product, strictly speaking it is not, because it is made from milk that has been inoculated with thermophilic cultures and then heated slightly. Sour milk products, on the other hand, are usually inoculated with lactic acid bacteria that become active at lower temperatures of around 68 °F (20 °C) (= mesophilic cultures).

The most well-known and traditional sour milk product is sour milk. This is formed if you leave raw milk in a warm room for a few days. The milk turns into sour milk when the lactic acid bacteria that are naturally present in the milk multiply. In days gone by, farmers would simply place deep dishes containing milk on a shelf just below the kitchen ceiling and leave them there for a while.

Alongside sour milk itself, sour milk products include sour cream and crème fraîche, each of which has a different fat content.

Homemade yogurt

Natural yogurt tastes particularly good with fruit.

Always check the temperature using a thermometer.

Whether you inoculate the yogurt with bought yogurt or a readymade yogurt culture depends on what you prefer to work with. Below are preparation methods for both variations.

Variation 1—with bought yogurt

Bought yogurt can contain different amounts of lactic acid bacteria. If when you open up the yogurt maker you can see that some whey has already settled, that is a sign that the lactic acid bacteria are very active. You should add slightly more or less than 1 tablespoon, depending on how sour the yogurt is.
When the animals are in the meadow or alpine pasture during the summer and eat a lot of fresh grass, the milk contains more active lactic acid bacteria. You will find this with bought yogurt too. If a yogurt has nearly reached its expiration date, more whey will settle on the surface.

Variation 2—with yogurt culture

If you would like to work with yogurt culture, see the packet instructions for quantities. You can find yogurt cultures in health stores, storehouses / agricultural suppliers, and on the internet.

How to make variations 1 and 2

▦ Place the milk in a pan and heat to 108 °F (42 °C) (use a thermometer). If you are using a yogurt culture, please refer to the instructions on the packet. Add either 1 tablespoon of yogurt or the culture to the milk, then stir thoroughly.

▦ Carefully pour the inoculated milk into the prepared yogurt jars, stirring all the time. Then screw the lids on the jars, place them in the yogurt maker, put the lid on, and switch on the machine. Make sure the yogurt maker is standing on a vibration-free surface.

▦ Now leave the milk to mature into yogurt by the action of heat, i.e. to incubate. After 4 to 5 hours, you should taste the yogurt. The yogurt is ready when it has formed a jellylike mass in the jars and has a typical yogurt taste. Taste the yogurt carefully, avoiding stirring in order to preserve the consistency. The yogurt will not become properly semisolid until later, in the fridge.

▦ Remove the finished yogurt from the yogurt maker immediately and place it in the fridge, otherwise it may become too sour. It is therefore important to plan your yogurt making to finish its incubating at a time when you are at home. Yogurt will keep in the refrigerator for 7 to 10 days. If the yogurt goes bad before this time, it is a sign that the bacteria have not developed as desired. In case of doubt, you should not eat the yogurt.

VARIATION 1
MAKES APPROX.
4 CUPS
(1 LITER)

4 cups (1 liter) milk
1 tbsp (15.5 g) sour
natural yogurt (semi-
solid, 3.6% fat)

VARIATION 2
MAKES APPROX.
4 CUPS
(1 LITER)

4 cups (1 liter) milk
yogurt culture

Greek yogurt

MAKES APPROX.
½ CUP (120 G)

1 cup (250 g) natural
yogurt

You can make Greek yogurt with either cow's or sheep's milk. Preparation is very easy. You can use readymade yogurt as the basis.

▦ Place a coffee filter over the edge of a jar or bowl and scoop the yogurt into it carefully, making sure the pores of the filter bag are not compressed, so the whey can drain off.

▦ After about 2 hours, turn the yogurt carefully using a spatula. This ensures the whey drains off evenly. The sourer the yogurt, the faster the whey will drain off.

▦ If the yogurt is very sour, the whey will drain off in 3 to 4 hours. If the yogurt is not very sour, you can leave the whey to drain off overnight.

To make cream yogurt, you can use a mixture of milk and cream at a ratio of 3:1.

Yogurt variations

For **goat's yogurt**, heat 4 cups (1 liter) of goat's milk to 108 °F / 42 °C and add 1 tablespoon of goat's yogurt. Stir vigorously. Pour into yogurt jars and leave to incubate in the yogurt maker for around 5 hours.

Vanilla yogurt is made from milk flavored with a hint of vanilla. Scrape the seeds from 2 vanilla pods, add to 4 cups (1 liter) of milk and stir vigorously. Allow the vanilla milk to cool for 1 day, then use it to prepare yogurt according to the basic recipe.

To make **sour milk**, heat the milk to a maximum 85 °F (30 °C) and leave to stand in a bowl in a warm place for 1 to 2 days. If you like, you can speed up the curdling of the milk by inoculating it with bought sour milk. Or you can follow the Danish example and place a bunch of yellow bedstraw in the milk, in order to stimulate the souring.

Yogurt with flowers

MAKES
1 PORTION

½ tsp vanilla sugar
½ cup (125 g) natural
yogurt
½ handful edible
flowers (St John's
wort, borage, holly-
hock, meadowsweet)

▧ Stir the vanilla sugar into the yogurt. Take some of the edible flowers and chop finely. Reserve the remaining flowers for decoration.

▧ Mix half of the chopped flowers into the yogurt. Sprinkle the other half on top of the yogurt together with the whole flowers to serve.

Coffee yogurt

MAKES
1 PORTION

generous ½ tsp
instant coffee
granules
½ tsp cocoa powder
1 tbsp boiling water
½ cup (125 g) natural
yogurt
sugar to taste
chocolate beans to
decorate

Instant powder is sometimes sweetened and if so does not require any additional sugar. You can prepare more coffee mixture than you need and store it in a screw-lid jar in the refrigerator, so you do not need to make fresh coffee mixture each time you want to make coffee yogurt.

▧ Stir the instant coffee granules together with the cocoa powder and the boiling water, then allow the mixture to cool. If you would like to sweeten the yogurt, add sugar to taste.

▧ Then stir the cooled coffee mixture into the yogurt and decorate the yogurt with chocolate beans.

TIP

For a change, you could try instant coffee in different flavors.

Apricot yogurt

MAKES
1 PORTION

4 very ripe apricots
½ cup (125 g) natural
yogurt
sugar to taste

▓ Wash, halve, and pit the apricots, then purée roughly in a food processor or with a hand blender. If you prefer the yogurt to be sweet, add sugar to taste.

▓ Cover the bottom of a glass bowl with a layer of apricot purée, layer the yogurt on top, and finish with the remaining apricot purée.

Variations

▓ You can prepare **other fresh fruit** of your choice in the same way. Stir the purée into the yogurt. Instead of puréeing the fruit, you can cut it into small cubes. Once you have mixed the yogurt with the fruit purée, you can freeze it in small ice pop molds. Or you could fill a large flat plastic container with the yogurt and place in the fridge for about 4 hours, stirring from time to time.

▓ Or you can mix the **yogurt with pear or apple purée**. Stir 2 tablespoons apple or pear purée into ½ cup (125 g) natural yogurt and flavor with cinnamon and vanilla sugar. If you like, you could add lemon balm leaves or a handful of chopped walnuts.

Muesli yogurt served two ways

VARIATION 1
MAKES
1 PORTION

½ cup (125 g) natural
yogurt
1–2 tbsp (15–30 g)
oats
1 tsp flax seeds

Nowadays, there is a wide variety of tasty, readymade mueslis available to buy. Nevertheless, it is worth bearing in mind that they often contain a relatively high quantity of sugar and are sometimes highly processed. If you like variety, you could make your own fresh muesli each day, using oats or crushed grain as a base. Why not try these two recipe suggestions?

▮ Stir the yogurt together with the oats and flaxseed or alternatively with swollen whole grain cereals.

Tip

VARIATION 2
MAKES
1 PORTION

Depending on the time of year, you could add your choice of fresh, finely chopped fruit, nuts, edible flowers, finely chopped spring herbs, pumpkin/sunflower seeds, and dried fruit such as prunes, figs, or raisins to the basic muesli and yogurt mixture.

½ cup (125 g) natural
yogurt
1 tbsp (12.5 g)
crushed grain
(swollen in water)

Hazelnut yogurt with syrup

MAKES
1 PORTION

generous ½ tsp
ground hazelnuts
½ cup (125 g) natural
yogurt
1 tsp chopped
hazelnuts
½ tsp molasses
some molasses to
decorate

▦ Stir the ground hazelnuts into the yogurt, add the chopped hazelnuts, and mix.

▦ Stir in the molasses. To decorate, dip a fork into the syrup jar, then drizzle a few threads of syrup over the yogurt.

Variations

▦ This recipe is similar to **Greek yogurt with walnuts** and honey. Break 1 tablespoon walnuts into small pieces and mix with ½ cup (125 g) Greek (cream) yogurt. If you like, you could drizzle 1 teaspoon honey over the yogurt in threads. Decorate with walnut halves to serve.

▦ Sesame also goes well with yogurt. Stir 1 teaspoon each of sesame paste (tahini) and honey into ½ cup (125 g) natural yogurt. Sprinkle with 1 teaspoon raw sesame seeds. Alternatively, fry the sesame seeds in butter and leave them to cool before sprinkling them.

TIP

The molasses will give the yogurt a nutty color and enhance the flavor of the hazelnuts.

Yogurt—health from the kitchen | 45

Cinnamon yogurt drink

MAKES
1 PORTION

¼ tsp cinnamon
1 tbsp sugar
6 tbsp (100 g) natural
yogurt
3–4 tbsp water

▓ Mix the cinnamon with the sugar and sprinkle onto a dessert plate. Damp the edge of the drinking glass to be used and dip it in the cinnamon and sugar mixture.

▓ Mix the yogurt with the water until smooth and stir in the rest of the cinnamon and sugar mixture. It is best to fill the glass only three-quarters full, then the sugared edge will be more visible.

Banana drink

MAKES
1 PORTION

½ banana
3–4 tbsp water
6 tbsp (100 g) natural
yogurt

▓ Peel the banana and purée it in a food processor or with a hand blender.

▓ Fold the banana purée and the water into the yogurt, and then give everything another mix.

VARIATIONS

You could use other fresh fruit such as raspberries, strawberries, apricots, or cherries. Simply wash, chop into small pieces, purée, and then mix with the yogurt to make a fruity drink.

Yogurt and lemon balm drink

MAKES
1 PORTION

1–2 tbsp lemon balm
syrup

▓ Add the lemon balm syrup to the yogurt (the syrup is available in shops selling herbal products, or you can make your own). Stir well, then add the mineral water. Serve immediately before the delicious yogurt froth subsides!

6 tbsp (100 g) natural
yogurt
7 tbsp (100 ml)
carbonated mineral
water

Green smoothies

MAKES
1 PORTION

1 handful wild herbs
(dandelion, nettle,
plantain) and young
garden herbs (lemon
balm, parsley, chives)
½ cup (125 g) natural
yogurt

In spring, nature positively invites us to pick fresh wild plants such as dandelion leaves and young stinging nettles and to make them into delicious smoothies. At this time of year, wild herbs have a strong diuretic effect and help to stimulate the metabolism, which, combined with yogurt, aids digestion. A one- to two-week course with breakfast drinks can do wonders for your vitality.

▓ Wash the wild and garden herbs, dab dry, and chop coarsely. Place in a food processor or use a hand blender to chop finely, then stir into the yogurt.

▓ If you like, you could also peel half a green apple, core, and purée it, and then stir the apple purée into the smoothie.

VARIATIONS

Over the course of the year, there are always new varieties of fresh fruit and vegetables you could add to these smoothies, such as asparagus in the spring, zucchini or cucumber in the summer, and cabbage in the autumn and winter.

Lassi

MAKES
2 GLASSES EACH
APP. 4 FL OZ
(125 ML)

½ cup (125 g) natural
yogurt
½ cup (125 ml) water
dash of lemon juice
1 pinch salt

Lassi is a refreshing yogurt drink from India. You can add all kinds of ingredients to it. The most well-known variation is lassi with cumin, but puréed fruits such as mango are also used.

▓ Place the yogurt in a food processor or mixing jug and gradually mix in the water, lemon juice, and salt. Pour the lassi into two glasses and serve immediately to enjoy the wonderful froth!

Ayran

MAKES
2 GLASSES EACH
APP. 4 FL OZ
(125 ML)

½ cup (125 g) natural
yogurt
5 tbsp (75 g) sour
cream

Like lassi, ayran is a traditional refreshment. It comes from the region of Anatolia and the Caucasus, which is further west.

▓ Place the yogurt and the sour cream in a food processor or mixing jug and mix well. Gradually add the water, lemon juice, and salt. Pour the ayran into two glasses and serve immediately.

½ cup (125 ml) min-
eral water or water
dash of lemon juice
1 pinch salt

Kefir—wellness from the Caucasus

Kefir can also be used to make cold beet soup.

I had heard a lot about the significant health benefits of kefir, but when I decided to try to find out more, I was immediately faced with the question of where to buy kefir grains. As I found out, kefir is not always easy to source locally but it is available via mail order. Of course, you might have a friend who ferments their own kefir grains and who can give you some.

But how is kefir made? Unlike other sour milk products, kefir grains contain yeast as well as lactic acid bacteria, which bind together to form a mold. If you add this mold (kefir starter) to milk and wait for 1–2 days, depending on the level of ripening required, you will be rewarded with delicious kefir. During the fermentation process, the lactose, the sugar present in milk, is largely broken down. People with lactose intolerance can therefore sometimes tolerate kefir. However, if you have this condition you should test this yourself, as everybody reacts differently.

Kefir is said to help you live to 100 if you consume it regularly. In the Caucasus people swear by its healing effects, and the significantly higher life expectancy of people who live in that part of the world is sometimes linked to the high consumption of kefir. Kefir is believed to have beneficial effects on the body in regulating blood pressure and aiding digestion. It is also said to contain antibiotic properties. Kefir that has ripened for up to 24 hours has a mild laxative effect on the intestine, while kefir that matures for about 48 hours has a more balancing effect.

Regular consumption of kefir is said to have a healing effect on depression and to counteract stress. However, this is based on hearsay and has not been proved scientifically—or at any rate has barely been proved. All the same, it is worth enjoying kefir as a very healthy food and deciding for yourselves. Incidentally, the origin of the word "kefir" is keif, a Turkish word stem which means something like "feel well / feel healthy." Please bear in mind that kefir contains between 0.2% and 2% alcohol, produced by fermentation of the lactose.

Fermenting your own kefir grains requires proper attention and care, as they dry out very quickly. If you look after them, the kefir grains will grow regularly and in a few weeks' time you can split the grains and give some to your friends.

Homemade kefir

Never use containers or equipment that are made of metal or that have metal components to make kefir, as this can have an adverse effect on the health of the grains. On the other hand, glass jars and chinaware are very suitable for making kefir. In addition, do not leave kefir in the sun while it is fermenting. It is best therefore either to cover the container with plastic wrap or to screw a lid onto it loosely, making sure some air reaches the contents.

Any type of milk is suitable for kefir. The proportion of fat does not matter.

Lemon and strawberry smoothie and blueberry kefir—irresistibly tasty and healthy!

MAKES APPROX. 4 CUPS (1 LITER)

1 tbsp kefir grains (exact amount will depend on experience and the mold used)
4 cups (1 liter) milk at room temperature

■ Place the kefir grains in a thoroughly clean glass and pour in the milk at room temperature. Then leave the kefir for about 24 hours in a shaded place at room temperature.

■ Pour the kefir through a plastic sieve into a glass or a bottle with a wide neck, seal the glass or bottle, and store in the refrigerator.

■ Carefully wash the leftover kefir grains in the sieve under cold, running water and then prepare your next batch.

Cold yogurt soup with baby gherkins

MAKES
4 PORTIONS

8 baby gherkins
1/3 cup (80 g) Feta
1/2 cup (125 g) sour cream
3 cups (750 g) natural yogurt
salt, pepper
ground caraway
pinch of paprika
1/2 slice bread
2 tbsp chopped chives

▥ Retain a half gherkin for decoration. Peel the remaining gherkins, and cut into slices. Purée the gherkin slices finely, either in a food processor or in a mixing jug using a hand blender.

▥ Gradually mix in the Feta, sour cream, and yogurt, and flavor the soup with salt, pepper, ground caraway, and paprika. Leave the soup to cool for about 1 hour.

▥ Spoon the soup into glass bowls. Cut the bread into small pieces and the remaining half gherkin into slices and use both to decorate. Sprinkle with the chives to serve.

Variation

▥ A similar dish is borscht, a cold kefir soup that is popular in Eastern Europe. It is made with beets and herbs, and sometimes served with radishes and eggs (see the photos on page 48).

Cold yogurt soup is perfect for hot summer days—try served with hearty farmhouse bread.

Raita

MAKES APPROX.
1 CUP (250 ML)

1/2 cucumber
1 cup (250 g) natural yogurt
salt, pepper
mint leaves to decorate

Raita has a cooling effect on the body and is therefore served alongside very hot dishes in Indian cooking. This variation with grated cucumber is particularly refreshing.

▥ Peel the cucumber and grate roughly. Place the grated cucumber in a sieve, leave to drain, and squeeze out any excess water.

▥ Place the grated cucumber in a bowl and stir together with the yogurt, salt, and pepper until smooth. Spoon into deep dishes and decorate with mint to serve.

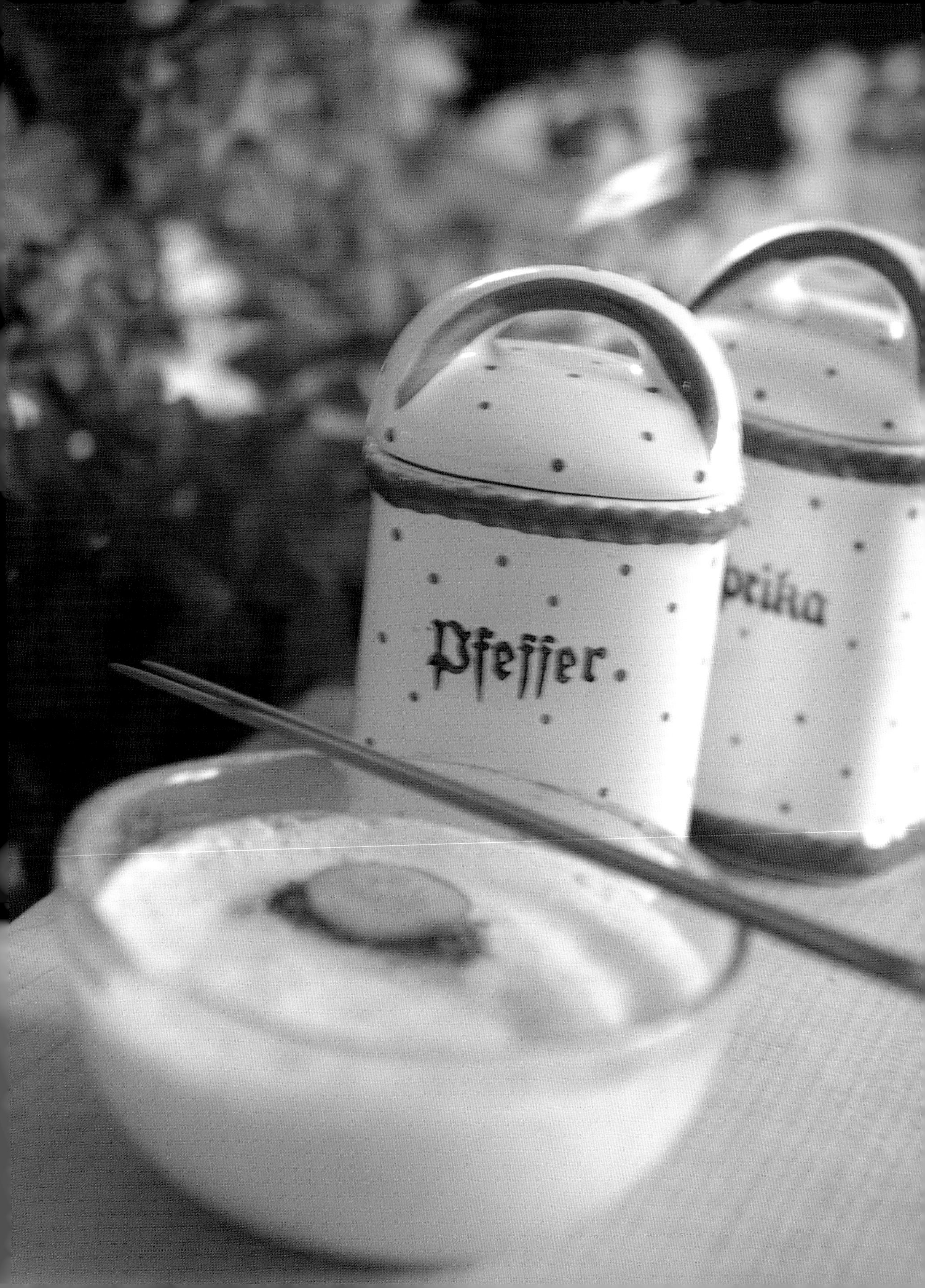
Pfeffer

Yogurt dressing with chanterelles

MAKES APPROX.
1 CUP (250 ML)

1 handful
chanterelles
½ onion
1 tsp butter
salt, pepper
1 tbsp chopped
parsley

▓ Wash the chanterelles, dab dry, and chop into small pieces. Peel the half onion and chop very finely.

▓ Heat the butter in a frying pan and fry the onion. Add the chopped chanterelles and season with salt and pepper.

▓ Fry the chanterelles for a few minutes. Drain off the juices. Leave the chanterelles to cool and then mix into the yogurt together with the chopped parsley.

1 cup (250 g) natural yogurt

Yogurt dressing with herbs

MAKES APPROX.
1 CUP (250 ML)

1 handful fresh
garden herbs (chives,
parsley, oregano,
thyme, marjoram)

▓ Wash the herbs, dab dry, and chop finely. Place the yogurt and the sour cream in a bowl, stir, then add the herbs. Season the dressing with salt and roughly ground peppercorns.

▓ Finally, cover the bowl with plastic wrap and leave the dressing to infuse for 1 hour in the refrigerator.

1 cup (250 g) natural yogurt
1 tbsp sour cream
salt, roughly ground peppercorns

Yogurt dressing with bacon and onions

MAKES APPROX.
1 CUP (250 ML)

½ small onion
1 tbsp oil
2 slices (50 g) bacon,
chopped

▓ Peel the onion half and chop very finely. Heat the oil in a frying pan and fry the onion and chopped bacon. Leave to cool.

▓ Mix the onion and bacon mixture with the yogurt, stir in the chopped parsley, and add salt according to taste.

1 cup (250 g) natural yogurt
1 tbsp parsley
salt to taste

Other yogurt dressings

With salmon

Left: Yogurt dressing
with chanterelles.
Right: With mustard
and anchovy paste,
with salmon, with
pumpkin seeds
(from front to back).

TIP

These yogurt sauces
go very well with
green leaf salads,
dumplings, cereal
patties, and roasted
vegetables, as well
as with fondues and
grilled meat.

Stir together 1 cup (250 g) natural yogurt, 1 tablespoon finely chopped smoked salmon pieces, and some roughly ground pepper. Decorate with nasturtium flowers to serve.

With mustard and anchovy paste

Stir together 1 cup (250 g) natural yogurt, 1–2 tablespoons hot mustard, ¼ teaspoon anchovy paste, and some chili flakes. Decorate with edible flowers such as borage to serve.

With pumpkin seeds

Stir together 1 cup (250 g) natural yogurt with 2 tablespoons chopped pumpkin seeds, 1 tablespoon pumpkin seed oil, salt, and pepper. Decorate with whole pumpkin seeds and edible St John's wort flowers to serve.

With cranberry jelly

Stir together 1 cup (250 g) natural yogurt with 1 tablespoon cranberry jelly and 1 tablespoon chopped parsley, then carefully fold in 1 tablespoon whipped cream.

Yogurt and cream gâteau with apricots

MAKES 1:
10 IN (26 CM)
SPRINGFORM
PAN

For the base
6 eggs
generous ¾ cup
(175 g) sugar
4 tbsp water
¼ tsp baking powder
1 cup (150 g) wheat
flour
fat and flour for pan

For the filling
1 cup (250 ml) cream
6 gelatin leaves
scant 1¼ cups
(300 g) nat. yogurt
5 tbsp (70 g) sugar

To decorate
1 cup (250 ml) cream
a few apricots
hazelnut brittle

▥ Preheat the oven to 375 °F (190 °C). To make the base, separate the eggs and beat the egg whites until stiff. Beat the sugar with the egg yolks and water until frothy.

▥ Sieve the baking powder with the flour and fold into the yolk mixture, alternating with the beaten egg whites. Grease the springform pan and dust with flour. Spread the mixture over the base of the pan and cook in the oven for 15–20 minutes. Remove and leave to cool in the pan.

▥ To make the filling, put 2 tablespoons (30 g) of the cream to one side and beat the rest of the cream until stiff. Soften the gelatin in cold water. Heat the 2 tablespoons of cream. Squeeze the water from the gelatin and dissolve in the warm cream. Leave to cool.

▥ Mix the gelatin cream together with the yogurt, sugar, and remaining cream. Spread the yogurt and cream mixture over the cooled base and leave the gâteau to cool for 3 hours.

▥ To decorate, remove the cake pan and whip the cream. Add the whipped cream to the gâteau, squirting on rosettes for decoration if required.

▥ Wash, halve, pit, and slice the apricots. Decorate the gâteau with apricot slices and sprinkle hazelnut brittle round the edge.

Yogurt, raspberry, and poppy seed gâteau

MAKES 1:
9 ½ IN (24 CM)
SPRINGFORM
PAN

For the base
8 eggs
¾ cup (170 g) soft
butter
¾ cup + 2 tbsp
(200 g) sugar
generous 3 cups
(300 g) ground
poppy seeds
1½ cups (140 g)
ground hazelnuts
¼ tsp cinnamon
fat and flour for pan

For the filling
1 cup (250 ml) cream
7 gelatin leaves
2 cups (500 g)
natural yogurt
¼ cup (55 g) sugar
2½ cups (250 g)
raspberries

▦ Preheat the oven to 340 °F (170 °C). Grease the springform pan and dust with flour. Separate the eggs and beat the egg yolks with the butter and sugar until frothy. Beat the egg whites until stiff and add to the sugar and butter mixture.

▦ Scatter the poppy seeds, hazelnuts, and cinnamon on top and fold in all the ingredients carefully using a spatula. Place the mixture in the springform pan, spread out until smooth, and bake in the oven for about 40 minutes. Remove and leave to cool.

▦ To make the filling, put 2 tablespoons (30 g) of the cream to one side and beat the rest of the cream until stiff. Soften 5 gelatin leaves in cold water. Heat the 2 tablespoons of cream in a small pan. Squeeze the water from the gelatin and dissolve in the warm cream. Mix together the yogurt, 3 tablespoons of the sugar, and the whipped cream. Stir in the dissolved, cooled gelatin. Spread the yogurt and cream mixture over the cooled base of the gâteau.

▦ Soften the remaining 2 gelatin leaves in cold water. Sort the raspberries, wash, and heat briefly in a small pan with 1 tablespoon sugar, stirring all the time. Leave to cool.

▦ Finally, squeeze the water from the gelatin and stir into the raspberry and sugar mixture. Scatter the raspberries over the yogurt cream and leave the gâteau to cool for several hours.

Tip

The raspberry gâteau would work equally well with a different base.

Bread with yogurt

MAKES 1:
7 IN (17 CM)
LOAF PAN

2 cups (300 g) rye
flour
1¹/₃ cups (200 g)
wheat flour
1 tsp flax seeds
1 tsp sunflower
seeds
1 tsp sesame seeds
¼ tsp mixed spice
2½ tsp salt
1 packet dry yeast
3 tbsp (45 g) sour
natural yogurt
1 cup (250 ml) hot
water
fat and flour for the
pan
hot, very weak filter
coffee to glaze
flour for dusting

I always make this bread in a mixing bowl that has a lid, so I can leave it to rise in the bowl. The lactic acid bacteria in the yogurt have a similar effect to sourdough on the rye flour and give the bread a pleasant sour taste.

▓ Mix the rye flour with the wheat flour in a bowl, together with the other dry ingredients. Whisk together the yogurt and the hot water and stir into the flour mixture. Knead the dough well, adding more flour if it is still too soft.

▓ Cover the dough and leave to rise in a warm place until it has doubled in volume. (If you want it to rise quickly, place the bowl in warm water.) Grease the pan and dust with flour.

▓ Split the dough into two halves. Shape one half into a rectangle and place in the loaf pan. Split the other half into three pieces, roll each piece into a strand, and weave the strands into a braid. Place the dough braid on the other half of the dough in the loaf pan and press down.

▓ Preheat the oven to 450 °F (230 °C). Brush the bread with hot filter coffee and dust with flour. This will give it a nice color and make it look like it has been baked in a wood-fired oven.

▓ Bake the bread in a preheated oven with a start temperature of 450 °F (230 °C), reducing the temperature to 375 °C (190 °C) after 5 minutes. The total baking time is 45 minutes. The bread is ready once it sounds hollow when you knock on it.

Tip

You can also shape the dough into small bread rolls or baguettes. Bake at the same temperature, for just 25–30 minutes.

White clay-pot bread

MAKES 1:
CLAY POT (6
IN / 15 CM IN
DIAM-ETER, 2 ¾
IN / 7 CM HIGH)

3 ⅓ cups (500 g)
wheat flour
2 tsp salt
1 packet dry yeast
¼ tsp ground
caraway
2 tbsp (30 g) natural
yogurt
1 cup (250 ml) hot
water
oil and flour for the
pot

▪ Place the flour, salt, dry yeast, and caraway together in a bowl and mix. Whisk the yogurt together with the hot water and stir into the flour mixture. Knead the dough thoroughly, adding more flour if it is still too soft.

▪ Cover the dough and leave in a warm place for about 30 minutes. When the volume of the dough has doubled, preheat the oven to 430 °F (220 °C).

▪ Grease the clay pot with oil and dust with flour. Knead the dough again briefly and press into the pot. Using a spatula, press a pattern onto the surface of the bread, and dust the surface with flour.

▪ Put the bread in the oven, turn the heat down to 350 °F (180 °C) and bake the bread for around 40 minutes. Immediately after baking, remove from the pot and leave to cool.

TIP

This dough is also suitable for small bread rolls or baguettes. The baking time is just 25–30 minutes.

Yogurt pot muffins

MAKES 12

4 eggs
1 pot oil
2 pots sugar
10 tbsp (150 g)
natural yogurt
(1 pot)
3 pots flour
¼ tsp baking powder
fat and flour for the
pans

Pot cakes are made without weighing. You measure most of the ingredients using a yogurt cup (for 10 tbsp / 150 g yogurt).

▓ Preheat the oven to 340 °F (170 °C). Grease the muffin pans and dust with flour. Place the eggs, oil, and sugar in a bowl and beat with a hand mixer until very frothy.

▓ Add the yogurt and stir well. Mix the flour with the baking powder and stir into the yogurt mixture.

▓ Place the mixture in the muffin pans and bake the muffins in the oven for around 25 minutes. Take the muffins out, leave to cool, and decorate with sugar, chocolate frosting, or punch icing if you wish.

You could also try making the muffins in small, oblong silicon cases.

Yogurt pot cake

MAKES 1:
10 ½ IN
(27 CM)
LOAF PAN

3 eggs
2 pots sugar
10 tbsp (150 g)
natural yogurt
(1 pot)
1 pot oil
3 pots flour
¼ tsp baking powder
2 tsp cocoa powder
fat and flour for the
pan

▓ Preheat the oven to 340 °F (170 °C). Place the eggs and sugar together in a bowl and beat with a hand mixer until very frothy. Add the yogurt and oil, and stir well. Sieve the baking powder with the flour and fold into the egg mixture.

▓ Grease the loaf pan and dust with flour. Spoon two-thirds of the mixture into the pan, stir the rest of the mixture together with the cocoa powder, and spoon over the lighter-colored mixture. Swirl a fork through both mixtures to form a marble pattern.

▓ Bake the cake in the oven for about 45 minutes. Take it out, transfer from the pan to a cake stand, and leave to cool.

Yogurt mousse with rose petals

MAKES
4 PORTIONS

5 gelatin leaves
1 cup (250 ml) cream
2 cups (500 g)
natural yogurt
2 tbsp (25–30 g)
sugar
1 tsp lemon juice
rose petals to
decorate

▓ Soften the gelatin in cold water. Put 2 tablespoons (30 ml) of the cream to one side. Beat the rest of the cream until stiff. Place the yogurt in a bowl together with the sugar and lemon juice, stir well. Heat the 2 tablespoons (30 g) cream in a small pan. Squeeze the water from the gelatin and dissolve in the warm cream, stirring all the time.

▓ Leave the gelatin cream to cool and then stir into the yogurt. Fold in the whipped cream carefully. Pour the mixture into small glass bowls and leave to cool for a few hours.

▓ To serve, tip the yogurt mousse from the bowls onto plates and cover the edge of each mousse with rose petals. If you like, you could decorate each mousse with a mallow flower.

TIP

Make sure the roses have not been sprayed—ideally use roses from your own garden!

Yogurt tiramisu

MAKES 4–6
PORTIONS

5 gelatin leaves
2 cups (500 ml)
cream
2 cups (500 g) semi-
solid natural yogurt
3 tbsp sugar
12 (200 g)
ladyfingers
1 cup (240 ml) hot
filter coffee (sweeten
if required)
cocoa for sprinkling

■ Soften the gelatin in cold water. Put 2 tablespoons (30 ml) of the cream to one side. Beat the rest of the cream until stiff and mix together with the yogurt and 3 tablespoons of sugar.

■ Heat the 2 tablespoons of cream in a small pan. Squeeze the water from the gelatin and dissolve in the warm cream, stirring all the time. Do not let the mixture get too hot. Leave to cool. Then stir the dissolved gelatin cream into the yogurt and cream mixture.

■ Cut the ladyfingers into pieces, dip into the coffee and layer side-by-side in an ovenproof dish. Spread one-third of the yogurt and cream mixture over the ladyfinger pieces, submerge the remaining ladyfingers in the coffee, and then layer them on top. Finish off with a layer of the remaining cream.

■ Leave the yogurt tiramisu to cool for around 3 hours. If you want it to cool faster, place in the freezer for 1 hour. Sprinkle with cocoa before serving.

Butter and cream— a taste sensation

Butter—historical and valuable

In many cultures, butter has a special place and is highly valued. In the ancient world, the Greeks and Romans used butter primarily for medicinal purposes. In the Middle Ages it became a sought-after trade item. Not only was it a valuable foodstuff, it was also used as packaging. For example, glasses were cast in butter so they could be transported safely without breaking. However, until 100 years or so ago, butter-making was extremely hard work. The cream was skimmed from milk bowls and then strenuously pounded or stirred in barrels by hand.

Great-grandma's bread and butter

For me, the delicious taste of butter brings back wonderful childhood memories. Sometimes in the afternoons, my friend and I would visit his great-grandma. Her bread and butter was something really special to us kids. I still remember how she spread the butter carefully on the bread and then handed it over as if it were something very precious. She loved having us visit to liven up her living room, and she gave us what she had. Now whenever I use butter, I always have a feeling of gratitude. Butter also always reminds me of baking, of delicious shortcrust pastry, and soft, melting puff pastry. When the smell of Christmas baking wafts through the house, the first thing I think of is Vanillekipferl cookies and shortbread—made with pure butter.

Respected in many cultures

Butter has a checkered past and opinions on its health benefits differ greatly. There are many voices in favor of enjoying butter, but there are also many people who are very critical of butter on health grounds. What do people in other parts of the world think of butter? In Asia and India, butter is used to make ghee, a type of clarified butter that is also known as the "gold of Ayurveda." Tibetan butter tea is also very interesting. It consists of black tea mixed with salt and yak butter and is traditionally drunk by monks. This combination is very nourishing and warming and therefore particularly suited to the high Tibetan altitudes. Apparently the layer of butter that forms at the top even keeps the tea warm. In days gone by, butter tea was considered a generous gift to a host or hostess as butter was a sign of wealth in Tibet. If we too think of butter as a delicious, valuable natural product that we should treat with care and respect, we shall be able to enjoy it ourselves.

Since butter-making used to be a manual and time-consuming task, butter was considered a very valuable foodstuff until the middle of the last century.

Butter and cream—some interesting facts

The basic product that is used to make butter is cream. For centuries, cream was obtained simply by leaving raw milk to stand. After a while, the milk would separate and the cream would form a solid layer on the top. Today, cream is separated from milk in dairies using a centrifuge.

Butter from the dairy

Cream is a so-called butter in water emulsion. Churning the cream separates the butter grains from the buttermilk.

In dairies, the cream is first pasteurized—a procedure that is not compulsory if you have made the cream yourself. In some areas butter sold on the farm direct to consumers also does not have to be pasteurized. After pasteurization, the cream is cooled again and either made straight into butter (sweet cream butter) or inoculated with lactic acid bacteria and left for about 20 hours (sour cream butter). It is good for the cream to rest for a day or two. This allows time for the butterfat to become evenly distributed and to form crystals.

To make butter, the fatty globules in the cream need to fuse together, so that the butter grains can exude. To help this process, the cream is beaten or stirred in vats or butter machines until buttermilk and butter grains are formed. The buttermilk is siphoned off and replaced by cold water. The butter is kneaded and the process is repeated two or three times, until all the buttermilk has been separated and removed. The butter is then shaped and packed.

Mildly soured butter (European-style butter) is made in the same way as sweet cream butter, with acidification cultures added later during churning. In alpine pastures, herdsmen and women and dairy workers produce **raw milk butter**.

Delicious buttermilk

The **buttermilk** that is produced after churning butter out of cream is good to drink and is particularly delicious as a cooling refreshment during the warm summer months. It is usually sour, either because it is a byproduct of the production of sour cream butter, or because it was soured later with acidification cultures (sweet cream butter). Due to its lactic acid bacteria content, it is suitable as a starter for yogurt and cheese-making. Buttermilk is relatively low in fat (max. 1% fat) and contains a large amount of protein.

What is butter made of?

To make 4½ cups of butter (1 kg), you need 3 quarts (2.5 liters) of cream. To obtain this amount of cream, you need to skim about 25 quarts (25 liters) of milk. You will understand therefore the high concentration of nutrients in butter, and why it was so valuable in days gone by—and continues to be popular today. This also means that, although butter is a

very high-quality foodstuff, we need to use it carefully and frugally in the interests of our health.

Fat is inherently the main ingredient in butter—fat that is obtained naturally. Butter contains at least 80% fat and in the US the fat content of most butters varies between 80 and 82%. In the EU, butter is divided into three categories according to its fat content:

Butter	80–90% fat (max. 16% water)
Three-quarter fat butter/reduced fat	60–62% fat
Half fat butter/light	39–41% fat

Butter contains the fat-soluble vitamins A, D, E, and K. The content level of these fat-soluble vitamins will depend on the fat content of the butter. Butter also contains significant amounts of calcium, potassium, and phosphorus, and very small quantities of lactose and protein. The nutritional content of butter has also been shown to depend on the animal feed. For instance, butter made from the milk of cows grazed in meadows or alpine pasture is usually more nutritious and has a yellow color because of the carotenoid contained in the feed. Coloring is usually added to industrially manufactured butter.

As mentioned above, opinions are divided about the quality of butterfat. There is no doubt that, as an animal fat, butter contains a relatively high amount of cholesterol. Nowadays, we know that a healthy person uses only a fraction of this cholesterol.

Delicate roses piped using freshly made buttercream. Keep chilled.

Moreover, butter contains predominantly saturated fatty acids and trans-fatty acids, of which we should limit our consumption. All the same, the fatty acids contained in butter are easily digestible, and not all trans-fatty acids from milk fat are bad for us.

The colorful world of butter

As well as classifying butter according to its fat content, different countries also categorize it according to closely defined grades and under names that do not enjoy protected status. As well as sensory characteristics such as appearance, smell, taste, and texture, features such as water content, spreadability, pH-value, and the microbiological properties of the butter also play their part.

Types of butter

In the USA, butter must contain at least 80% butterfat. European butters have up to 85%. **Sweet cream butter** is made from pasteurized fresh cream, with bacterial cultures and lactic acid. Before modern production methods arrived, cream collected from several milkings was used to make **cultured butter**. In Europe, butter is still sometimes made from fresh or cultured unpasteurized cream and is known as **raw cream butter**. It lasts for about ten days in a refrigerator. Most other types keep for several months.

Sweet cream butter is preferred in the USA and the UK. In continental Europe cultured butter is favored. It is sometimes labeled "European-style" in the USA, where commercial raw cream butter is rarely available.

All types of butter are sold both salted and unsalted. Spreadable butters are available too. They remain soft at cold temperatures.

Other cream products

Cream is not just processed into butter. It is also the basis for sour cream, crème fraîche, and so on, and also a popular foodstuff in its own right, whether whipped or for pouring. Obtaining cream is quite easy. If you leave raw milk to stand for a few hours, the cream will form a layer on the top and can be skimmed off. A certain amount of instinct is required to be able to skim the cream at the right consistency to ensure it will be suitable for whipping later on.

Cream has many uses—whether for decorating tarts, enhancing purées, flavoring sauces and soups, or whipping to serve with cake. Incidentally, the higher the fat content in the cream, the more stable and solid it will be if whipped.

There are also two basic types of cream. Light (or single) cream has to contain a minimum of 10% fat, whipping cream a minimum of 30% fat. Cream is also pasteurized through heat treatment and ultra-high heat treatment. Nowadays, you can find numerous cream-like products that claim to offer the same taste with fewer calories in the supermarket chiller aisle. Whether this promise holds true is for you to decide. Many countries have different cream products such as crème double, double cream (40–55% fat), and clotted cream (min. 55% fat).

Sour cream, heavy sour cream, and so on

If you inject cream (mixed with milk) with lactic acid bacteria, in a few hours' time you will have another wonderful dairy product: sour cream, which is one of the sour milk products. It has a slightly more solid consistency than cream and is good for enhancing dishes. Sauces made from sour cream should be heated only gently and not boiled. Crème fraîche, on the other hand, can be stirred into boiling sauces without it curdling.

The following cream products can be classified according to their fat content:

United States	Fat content (%)	United Kingdom
	55	Clotted cream
	48	Extra-thick double cream
Heavy cream	36+	
	35	Whipping cream, whipped cream
Light whipping cream	30–36	
	23	Sterilized cream
Light cream	18–30	
	18	Cream, single cream
	12	Half cream, sterilized half cream
Half cream	10.5–18	

Homemade butter

It is very easy to make butter at home, and the result is a tasty butter that is free from additives. For the recipes on the following pages, be sure to use good-quality cream as the starting product. Fresh creams that are as natural as possible are particularly suitable. Long-life cream can also be used, although the taste is compromised. If you make your butter from cream that has been heat treated, you can expect it to last longer. The butter will also have more of a neutral taste, which can be an advantage if it is to be processed further. Sheep's and goat's cream are also suitable for butter-making.

You can make butter in your own kitchen quite easily, using a food processor, a hand mixer, or an old-fashioned hand crank for whipping cream. Or you can buy a small butter-churning machine—this is definitely worthwhile if you intend to make all your own fresh butter. You are sure to have discovered how easy it is to make butter if you have ever beaten cream for too long and a few butter grains have formed.

Sweet cream butter

MAKES APPROX.
⅔ CUP (150 G)

2 cups (500 ml)
cream (min. 30% fat)

If you skim the cream from the raw milk yourself, take care to skim the layer of cream as horizontally as possible, and to avoid removing milk at the same time. Otherwise the cream will have a watery consistency and will be difficult or impossible to whisk later.

▥ Beat or churn the cream (with the mixer, a hand crank, or a butter churn) until the buttermilk separates from the butter grains.

▥ To wash the butter, drain off the buttermilk, measure it in a measuring jug, and add the same amount of cold water to the butter. Continue to beat or churn the butter for as long as buttermilk continues to separate.

▥ Finally, knead the butter mass into a brick shape or spread it into molds. If you are going to store it in the refrigerator, wrap it in plastic wrap or greaseproof paper.

Sour cream butter

Makes approx.
⅔ cup (150 g)

2 cups (500 ml)
cream (min. 30% fat)
2 tbsp (30 g) natural
yogurt (3.6% fat)

Because of its higher lactic acid bacteria content, sour cream butter keeps for longer than sweet cream butter and is less sensitive to foreign bacteria and odors. Nevertheless, it does not have a neutral taste like sweet cream butter, because the typical butter flavor is formed during the ripening process.

▥ Mix the cream with the yogurt in a china bowl and leave to stand for about 24 hours at room temperature. Then follow the same steps as for making sweet cream butter.

Tip

If you are making a small quantity of butter, say about 2¼ cups (500 g), you do not need to wash the butter again. If you are making a larger quantity of butter, drain the water off two or three times, and replace it with fresh water, then knead the butter again.

A greeting from the kitchen

Butter is a premium basic product that you can use to make many variations, such as butter with herbs and spices or butter with anchovies, salmon, caviar, or lemon. Why not offer this small greeting from the kitchen with some bread before the meal, or with the meat dish if it is herb butter, or with the fish course, depending on the flavored butter variation?

Herb butter

MAKES APPROX.
7 TBSP (100 G)

2 handfuls herbs
(parsley, chives)
7 tbsp (100 g) butter
salt

▦ Wash the herbs, dab dry, then chop roughly. Place in the mixer and chop finely. Add the butter and salt and mix everything thoroughly. Place the herb butter on small glass plates and serve with fresh bread.

Tip

You can also add salt or dried herbs such as marjoram, thyme, and caraway to the butter. Then divide into 1 generous tablespoon (10–20 g) portions. Freeze. The butter will absorb the flavor of the herbs and spices very easily. The frozen butter pieces are perfect for enhancing sauces. Simply stir in about 10 minutes before the end of the cooking time.

Flavored butter variations

Lemon butter

Take a half raw lemon, cut a slice from it, then peel and chop the slice finely. Squeeze the juice from the rest of the half lemon. Place the butter and the lemon juice in the mixer, mix until creamy, then add the lemon pieces and mix briefly.

TIP

To enhance your butter, remove it from the refrigerator 10–15 minutes before processing.

Anchovy butter

Drain generous 1 tablespoon (20 g) anchovies and chop in the mixer. Add 7 tablespoons (100 g) butter and mix until creamy.

Salmon butter

Drain a small can (100 g) of smoked salmon and chop in the mixer briefly. Add 8½ tablespoons (125 g) butter and mix. Finally, add some chopped parsley.

Tuna butter

Drain 1 small can of tuna. Peel and chop a half onion. Mix the tuna and the onion in the mixer, add 8½ tablespoons (125 g) butter, and mix until fluffy.

Beurre maître d'hôtel

Mix 8½ tablespoons (125 g) butter in the food processor until light and fluffy. Add 1 teaspoon strong mustard, 1 tablespoon chopped parsley, and salt and pepper. Mix well.

Wild garlic butter

Wash and sort 1 handful wild garlic leaves, chop in the mixer. Mix in 8½ tablespoons (125 g) butter. Lightly sprinkle with salt. (1 handful of watercress would also work well.)

Butter art—wooden molds

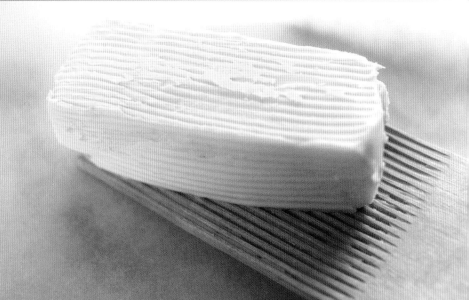

Fresh butter that has been shaped beautifully in a wooden mold—a treat for the eyes and the taste buds alike.

In the alpine regions of Switzerland, Germany, and Austria, there is a charming tradition that reflects the high regard in which butter is held. It is the use of hand-carved wooden molds to portion the butter. This enables producers to present their butter in a manner befitting its value.

Beautifully cut molds

The beautiful molds are mostly cut from maple. Nowadays, it is hard to find examples of this craftsmanship outside the alpine region. The wooden molds are decorated with typical motifs, ranging from suns and hearts to decorative ornaments. They also feature traditional motifs with an agricultural theme, such as grain, flowers, and cattle.

In the past, people who did not make their own butter but bought it as a large block would often use wooden butter molds at home to shape handy meal-size portions from the large butter blocks, and to present them in an attractive way.

How do you get the butter out again?

Before filling the wooden butter mold, soak it in water for about 30 minutes. Then fill the mold with the soft butter using a spatula, ensuring it is as airtight as possible. Press the butter in firmly. Scrape the rest away, cover the mold with plastic wrap, and place in the refrigerator for a few hours to cool. To get the butter out of the mold, turn the mold upside down and tap it gently on the work surface.

Butter molds and stamps were traditionally made by specialist wood-carvers, just like other wooden kitchen equipment.

Roll molds, stamps, folding molds

There are many other techniques for molding butter into decorative shapes. You can roll the butter over a mold board or imprint decorations using roll molds. Special butter stamps enable you to portion the butter and to decorate it at the same time—they also make it easy to remove a butter portion. The butter can be shaped using a folding mold with several parts. You can find ceramic and silicon butter molds, and butter can of course be easily shaped in small baking pans.

Ghee—clarified butter

Ghee is similar to concentrated butter and is part of traditional Ayurvedic cuisine in India. During the production of ghee, the butterfat separates from the protein and lactose in butter, and the water evaporates so that ghee is nearly 100% pure butterfat. If ghee is made properly, it is generally suitable for people who are lactose intolerant.

In Ayurvedic medicine, ghee is said to have healing properties, and it is held in high regard. It is thought to bind with free radicals in the body and render them powerless. Ghee is also believed to help the body absorb healing herbs. Homemade ghee requires particular patience and instinct. Use 4½ cups (1 kg) of butter to make generous 3 cups (700 g) of ghee.

Concentrated butter is made like ghee (with a slightly shorter cooking time) and has similar characteristics. It is exceptionally good for baking and frying.

TIP

Ghee is very good for frying and baking, and can be flavored, for example with caraway, cinnamon, garlic, or seasoning salt. I enjoy ghee on its own. Simply spread a thin layer on some bread and enjoy!

Homemade ghee

MAKES APPROX.
1 ½ CUPS
(350 G)

2¼ cups (500 g) butter

■ Place the butter in a pan and melt gently. Carefully skim the foam that appears on the top layer, until the butter has clarified. Do not scrape the solids that collect on the bottom of the pan. Pour the finished ghee into preserving jars. It will keep in the refrigerator for a few months.

Ghee muesli bars

MAKES APPROX.
25 BARS

14 tbsp (200 g) ghee
2¼ cups (200 g) oats
¼ cup (40 g) sesame seeds
½ cup (40 g) ground flax seeds
4 tsp honey

■ Melt the ghee gently in a pan. Stir in the oats, sesame, flax seeds, and honey. Remove the pan from the heat, and leave everything to swell for 10 minutes.

■ Cover a baking sheet with baking paper and spread the mixture over it. Using a knife, cut the bars into the desired size and shape. Push the mixture apart slightly at the intersections. Flatten the bars with the back of the knife and leave to cool for about 3 hours.

VARIATIONS

You can add small pieces of dried fruit or chopped nuts to the ghee bars.

Panna cotta with caramel sauce

MAKES
4 PORTIONS

2 gelatin leaves
2 cups (500 ml)
cream (min. 30% fat)
3 tsp sugar
seeds from ½ vanilla
pod
7 tbsp (100 g) fine
granulated sugar
7 tbsp (100 ml) water

This is traditional Italian cuisine, and this dessert is also very popular in countries outside Italy. The difficulty in making panna cotta is getting the right ratio of cream to gelatin. The longer you cook the cream, the less gelatin you need.

▦ Soften the gelatin in cold water. Simmer the cream, sugar, and vanilla seeds gently in a pan while stirring. Then squeeze the water from the gelatin and stir into the warm cream. Pour the gelatin cream into prepared ramekins, cover, and place in the refrigerator for a few hours to cool.

▦ To make the caramel, heat the sugar in a pan, and stir until the sugar starts to caramelize. Reduce the heat and continue to stir the caramel until it is a brown color and has a pleasant smell.

▦ Remove the pan from the heat and stir in the water. Cook the caramel sauce for a further 3 minutes while stirring constantly. Then pour the sauce into a preserving jar and leave to cool. To serve, pour the caramel sauce over the panna cotta.

You could also add …

… Raspberries: Wash and dab dry 2 cups (200 g) fresh raspberries. Place the raspberries on plates and tip the panna cotta out of their ramekins next to the raspberries. Decorate with chocolate flakes. Depending on the season, blueberries, cherries, and blackberries also go well with this dish.

… Orange slices: Peel 1 orange and cut into slices. Place the orange slices on dessert plates and tip the panna cotta out of their ramekins next to the orange slices. To serve, drizzle the panna cotta with orange liqueur.

TIP

You can serve the panna cotta straight from the ramekin. Or loosen the panna cotta from the edge of the ramekin with a knife and transfer it to a dessert plate.

Homemade ice cream

Making ice cream without an ice-cream maker takes a bit more effort. You will be rewarded with a smooth, melt-in-the-mouth dessert!

▓ Heat the cream slightly and stir in the sugar. Pour into a plastic bowl, cover, and place in the freezer for about 30 minutes.

▓ Scrape the ice away from the edge and stir the mixture well for about 2 minutes. Repeat this process once an hour for the next 3 hours, until the ice cream is frozen through and creamy.

▓ Lastly, add the jelly and stir the ice cream again. Continue stirring until the ice cream is creamy, then serve immediately.

Mascarpone

**MAKES APPROX.
2 CUPS (500 G)**

8½ tbsp (120 g)
butter
7 tbsp (100 ml)
cream (min. 30% fat)
1 cup (250 g) quark
(20% FiDM)

Mascarpone is a fresh cheese with a very high fat content. Here is a recipe for a simple type of mascarpone that does not require cheese-making or curdling.

▓ Melt the butter carefully in a pan, taking care that it does not get too hot. Pour in the cream and heat the mixture until the temperature reaches 115 °F (46 °C) (use a thermometer). Then stir in the quark, spoon the mascarpone into glasses, and chill.

INFO

Mascarpone, a specialty of the Lombardy region, is the main ingredient in the popular Italian dessert tiramisu.

Crème fraîche

**MAKES APPROX.
2 CUPS (500 G)**

2 cups (500 ml)
cream (min. 30% fat)
2 tbsp buttermilk

I always make crème fraîche (and sour cream) in my yogurt maker. That way it is easy to keep the temperature constant. If you are making only small quantities, you can simply fill the other glasses in the yogurt maker with warm water. Or you can make sour cream or yogurt at the same time …

▓ Carefully heat the cream up to 90 °F (32 °C) (use a thermometer) in a pan. Stir in the buttermilk and pour the mixture into the yogurt jars. Place the jars in the yogurt maker and leave to incubate for 12 hours. Then place in the fridge.

Sour cream

MAKES APPROX.
2 CUPS (500 G)

1 cup (250 ml) full-fat
milk
1 cup (250 ml) cream
(min. 30% fat)
2 tbsp buttermilk

▦ Stir the milk and cream in a pan and carefully heat to 90 °F (32 °C) (use a thermometer). Stir in the buttermilk and pour the mixture into small jars. Place the jars in the yogurt maker and leave to incubate for 12 hours. Then place in the fridge.

Warm sour cream sauces

These sauces go well with pasta. However, you can also serve them with vegetarian dishes such as spelt or millet patties. When heating the sour cream, take care not to heat it too much, otherwise it will curdle.

Herb sauce

Gently heat $2^2/_3$ cups (500 g) sour cream, taking care it does not get too hot. Add 1 handful of chopped herbs such as parsley, chives, and oregano to taste, and also salt if wished.

Gorgonzola sauce

Gently heat $1^1/_3$ cups (350 g) sour cream, taking care it does not get too hot. Add generous 1 cup (120 g) crumbled Gorgonzola into small pieces and dissolve the Gorgonzola in the sour cream while stirring continuously.

Cold sour cream dressings

Mix 1 cup (250 g) of sour cream with any of the following ingredients:
▦ 1 handful chopped herbs
▦ 1 small can tuna, drained and puréed
▦ 1 teaspoon each of ketchup and mayonnaise
▦ ½ cucumber, peeled, finely grated, and squeezed
▦ 100 g ham, cut into fine strips

Quark—
fresh cheese
made easy

1001 types of cheese —from fresh to hard

Nowadays there is an unbelievable variety of cheeses to choose from. They can be classified according to their texture and the style of manufacture, but they are often officially classified into groups according to their water or their fat content.

The table below gives a general idea of how commercial cheeses are differentiated by **water content**. There are seven broad groups, and the percentages shown are approximate. The divisions between "soft," "semisoft," "semihard," and "hard" are inexact, and many types of cheese are available both in soft and firm versions.

Fresh cheese:	more than 73% water
Soft cheese:	more than 67% water
Sour milk cheese:	60–73% water
Semisolid semihard cheese:	61–69% water
Semihard cheese:	54–63% water
Hard cheese:	maximum 56% water

Those who enjoy eating cheese often want to know about the **fat content**. The following list gives an idea of what fat content to expect. Some cheeses are available with a choice of fat content:

Low fat:	Up to 10%
Half fat:	11–20%
Three-quarters fat:	21–30%
Full fat:	40%

The simplest way to classify cheese is into "fresh" cheese and cheese that has "ripened" for more or less time.

There is also an important distinction to be made according to the type of curdling that takes place. In quark and cheese production, different amounts of rennet and acidification cultures are added. Fresh cheese and quark solidify primarily through the addition of an acidification culture and little to no rennet. Soft, semihard, and hard cheese, however, solidify primarily through the addition of rennet and very little acidification culture.

The lowdown on quark

Quark production is cheese-making in the broadest sense. Quark is the simplest kind of cheese, and the first step in cheese-making. Bacteria in the air cause milk to curdle, the mass is sieved, and then left to mature for a short or longer period of time. The history of quark goes back as far as antiquity, when quark recipes were already being handed down.

From Cato to Kneipp

Fresh cheese
has been made
according to the
same principle for
hundreds of years.
You leave the milk
to curdle and then
drain it in a special
cloth.

In ancient Rome, Cato the Elder (234–149 BC) described a recipe with quark as the basis for a cake. According to the recipe, quark was formed when the whey drained off sour milk contained in a cloth.

Nowadays, quark and fresh cheese are widespread in those regions that were once settled by the Romans, whether in the form of formaggio fresco in Italy, fromage blanc in France, or quark in Austria. What is striking about quark is that it features as an ingredient in a wide variety of dishes in different European cuisines, for example cheesecake in northern Germany, potato spread in Austria, and paskha in Russia (see the photo on page 7).

Incidentally, although Father Sebastian Kneipp (1821–1897) is most commonly associated with hydrotherapy, he was an advocate of quark and recommended it as a very valuable foodstuff, particularly for children. Kneipp treated thousands of patients, healing many of them, and recognized even then the connection between health and the nutritional value of dairy products.

Homemade with love

The German saying *So ein Topfen/Quark* (What baloney) dates from a time when quark was not very highly respected. I can still remember when our eldest daughter went to school 25 years or so ago. At the time, making your own dairy products was frowned upon and associated with being mean. The idea was that if something did not cost anything, it was not worth very much! Homemade dairy products were increasingly being replaced by industrially produced products.

Times have changed. Nowadays, if you offer guests fine quark spreads, flavorsome quark balls, or a light and creamy cheesecake, you can be sure of a positive and appreciative response. As homemade products grow in popularity, so too does quark. A pleasing development! This pleasure makes up for the (slight) increase in work.

Culinary allrounder

Quark tastes very good on its own, and is also a popular ingredient for spreads, quark dishes, sauces, pastries, pies, and cakes. It is a valuable source of protein.

Quark has many uses in the kitchen, whether for spreads, cakes, or fruit creams. It is often used to help bread and baked goods rise. Because of the high lactic acid content of quark, baked goods that contain quark are particularly light and creamy and rise very well. Quark can also be used a basic ingredient for various types of dough, such as quark puff pastry and semolina dumplings with quark.

You can preserve spicy quark balls in good-quality oil, a sinfully good flavor combination! Fresh cream cheese is good for thickening soups and sauces. Low fat quark makes a good spread for bread if you are trying to cut down on calories. In our house, quark is one of those foods that we always have in stock. Its versatility has made us big quark fans.

Valuable protein

Like all dairy products, quark has its place in our nutrition. On average, quark contains 10–12% protein, and about 4% carbohydrate and 0.1–4% fat. Given that its water content is still 80% even after the whey has drained off, 4 cups (100 g) of quark provide just 67–97 calories.

Quark is rich in potassium, calcium, and phosphorus, and far more nutrient dense than yogurt. While 3 quarts (3 liters) of milk will produce 3 quarts (3 liters) of yogurt, the same amount of milk will produce just 2 to 3½ cups (500 to 900 g) of quark.

Quark is a good source of protein for vegetarians in particular. It is especially good for health when combined with potatoes as the proteins in both foods complement each other perfectly. No wonder that some European adverts for quark used to say it was "as valuable as a small steak" to children.

Cooling remedy

I can still remember that our mother used to swear by a quark pack for mucus coughs. Even today, in Germany quark is used in hospitals to soothe mastitis after childbirth. Many doctors also recommend it to treat injuries after accidents. Quark is a tried-and-tested household remedy for external use, which is also recognized in natural healing. Its healing effects are based partly on its cooling properties when it is applied cold—it helps to reduce inflammation and fever. On the other hand, it draws contamination from the skin, a bit like medicinal clay. Although quark can put a stop to inflammation, it should not be applied to open wounds. Quark packs are particularly beneficial for treating minor sunburn and insect bites. I simply spread the quark on muslin or a clean dish towel and place it on the affected body part.

All about production

You can make quark with nearly every type of milk. Although natural milk produces a more intense flavor, fresh pasteurized milk still produces very good quark. If you use ESL or UHT milk, however, the boiled flavor may be recognizable in the end product. You can use either full fat milk or skim milk, depending on the amount of fat you would like to have in the quark.

Starters

Different starters in the form of lactic acid cultures, buttermilk, or yogurt will give the end product its individual character. Once the milk has been heated to the desired temperature, buttermilk or yogurt is added as a starter culture. Or you can add bought cultures. The lactic acid bacteria from the cultures break the lactose down into lactic acid, which makes the milk protein curdle. The addition of rennet speeds up the process.

Rennet from the laboratory

Rennet is a mixture of enzymes that occurs naturally only in the so-called fourth stomach of mammals. Nowadays it can also be derived from microorganisms. Animal rennet is available in liquid form or as tablets or powder. Rennet causes the milk protein to condense and the whey to separate from the curds (curdling). After this, the milk mass is called the "coagulum."

Adding rennet will increase the amount of quark produced and achieve a milder taste. If you are making quark at home, choose a liquid rennet which has instructions for using with small quantities of milk.

Rennet is a very sensitive product. Therefore it is best always to follow the instructions on the packet. If you use too much rennet, this may limit the development of the lactic acid bacteria, in which case the whey that drains off will be yellowish rather than greenish, the quark will be crumbly, and the sour flavor will be missing. You can nevertheless still make fresh soft cheese from this coagulum.

Handkäs mit Musik (handmade sour milk cheese with onion garnish)

It is also possible to make quark without cheese rennet, in which case the quark will taste sourer. The yield will be much smaller too. The sour milk quark produced in this way is relatively dry and can be used as a base product for sour milk cheese, which is particularly popular in central Germany.

If you mix the sour milk quark (made from skim milk) with salt and spices, shape it into the traditional patties, and leave it to ripen, you will end up with cheeses such as the ones named Harzer, Mainzer, and Korbkäse. The best-known dish using this is Handkäs mit Musik, a hand-shaped sour milk cheese that is traditionally served in an onion vinaigrette.

Cheesecloths, curd cloths, and so on

To drain off the whey, the quark is scooped into a cheesecloth or curd cloth. You can also use curd bags, but I find the cloths more practical as you can knot and hang them easily. They are also easier to clean than curd bags. Please make sure you only use proper cheesecloths or curd cloths! Cloths with larger or smaller weaves will make it more difficult for the whey to run off. If the quark curds have an optimal consistency, the whey will drain away very quickly. If the drainage is slow and impeded from the start, that may be a sign of a problem with the product.

A typical Hessian snack: Handkäs mit Musik (handmade sour milk cheese with onion garnish) with bread and butter and cider.

Even as you make your delicious quark, you can be thinking about how you intend to use it. This is because the quark will have a different consistency depending on how long you leave it to drain in the cheesecloth. For quark balls, for example, the quark should be on the dry side, so it is easy to work with later on. For a drier quark, simply leave the whey to drain away for a bit longer. If you are using store-bought quark to make quark balls, you can also hang this quark in a cheesecloth to drain.

Just as with yogurt, you should always use a thermometer when making all kinds of cheese. A cheese harp, a large knife, a spatula, and possibly a whisk, are also useful. It is a good idea to have separate crockery and utensils that you only use for dairy processing. If the quark does not turn out well, it is best to boil all the equipment that has been used. It is not enough just to use hot tap water as some bacteria are very heat resistant.

Sample the product

As with all homemade dairy products, it is best to smell and taste the quark at regular intervals. It should have a pleasantly sour to mild smell, depending on the acidification ingredient used. If there is whitish whey swimming on the top of the quark, for example, this usually suggests abnormal fermentation with yeast in the air. The product is no longer edible and should be thrown away.

Storage and recipes

Like all dairy products, quark should never be left uncovered as it will easily absorb other aromas. If you cannot use the whole amount at once, quark freezes well.

Try different fat contents to see which taste you prefer and which is easiest to work with. For cake and pastry fillings with cream, I use half fat quark. For puff pastry I use half fat quark or homemade full fat quark. Quark with a higher fat content tends to taste lighter and creamier and almost to melt in the mouth, while quark with a lower fat content is crumblier and tastes sourer. If you use quark with a higher fat content, any products you make—for example, spreads—will have a more intense flavor. This is because fat is a flavor carrier and enhancer, as mentioned above.

In the recipe section, you will find many suggestions for quark dishes. If you make your own quark, I am sure you will be particularly happy to discover new ways to enjoy quark. When I first began to make quark many years ago, I was always on the lookout for new recipes and ways to make this delicious natural product even better.

You can buy special cheesecloths and curd cloths from specialist cheese-making suppliers. They have the right weave for whey drainage. They should be boiled after each cheese-making session.

Homemade quark

Enhance your homemade quark with sweet or spicy ingredients.

You can make quark from skim and full fat milk. Below are two quark variations, one made with rennet and one without.

Variation 1—with rennet

MAKES
3–3 ½ CUPS
(800–900 G)

3 quarts (3 liters) milk
½ cup (125 ml buttermilk) (or corresponding amount of culture)
rennet (about ⅓ of the quantity for cheese according to the instructions on the packet)

▓ Heat the milk to 90 °F (32 °C) (use a thermometer) in a large pan and add the buttermilk or culture. Stir well and turn off the heat. Remove from the heat and stand the mixture close to the warm stove for about 30 minutes, or wrap in a dish towel. During this time, the lactic acid bacteria will develop very quickly.

▓ Then mix the rennet with some water and stir into the milk mixture using a whisk. Finally, bring the milk to a standstill with a counter movement of the whisk.

▓ Continue as for variation 2, starting at step 2.

Variation 2—without rennet

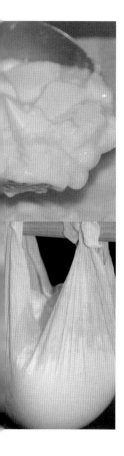

▦ Heat the milk to 90 °F (32 °C) (use a thermometer) and add the buttermilk or culture. Stir well.

▦ Place the pan containing the milk mixture in a warm place, such as near a radiator or on top of a refrigerator that gives off heat. Or you can put the pan in an oven that has been preheated to 120 °F (50 °C) and turned off again. After about 24 hours, a greenish whey will start to settle at the top as the lactic acid bacteria grow. Also the curdled milk will separate from the edge of the pan and congeal.

▦ Taste the quark at regular intervals. This will help you know when to skim. It can take up to two days for the milk to solidify, depending on the activity of the lactic acid bacteria, the warmth, and other influences (e.g. the weather).

▦ To skim the coagulum, score it with a knife or cut with a cheese harp. Leave to stand for another 30 minutes so part of the whey can be drained off.

▦ Then scoop the quark curds carefully into a cheesecloth (or curd cloth) that has been rinsed in cold water and placed in a large sieve (see the top picture). By gently moving the ends of the cloth to and fro, you will get more whey to drain off.

▦ Knot the ends of the cloth and hang it on a suitable wooden stick (see the bottom picture). Suspend over a container to catch the whey. Move the cheesecloth to and fro several times and scrape the dry quark away from the edges with a spatula, so the whey can continue to run off.

▦ Once the quark has fully separated from the whey, place it in a sealable bowl and chill. For a very smooth end product, sieve the quark. Then rinse the cheesecloth immediately in cold water before boiling.

FOR APPROX.
2 CUPS (500 G)

3 quarts (3 liters) milk
½ cup (125 ml) buttermilk (or corresponding amount of culture)

Info

Schichtkäse is a type of quark made in Germany that is not stirred or centrifugalized before packaging, but cut and placed in plastic tubs in layers. It is usually a bit meatier and more solid than quark.

Homemade fresh cream cheese

Fresh cream cheese contains significantly more fat than quark and therefore has a more full bodied taste.

To make fresh cream cheese, simply follow the basic quark recipe using 3 quarts (3 liters) of full-fat milk, and add 1 cup (250 ml) of cream to the milk. This fresh cheese has a high fat content, but is easily spreadable and very popular as a spread for bread (simply season with salt and pepper).

Tzatziki

MAKES APPROX.
2 CUPS (500 G)

2 garlic cloves
½ cucumber
1 cup (250 g) fresh cream cheese
6 tbsp (100 g) natural yogurt
salt, roughly ground pepper

▥ Peel the garlic cloves and chop finely. Peel the cucumber and grate roughly, then drain the grated cucumber in a sieve and squeeze out well.

▥ Mix the fresh cream cheese and yogurt together and season with a pinch of salt and roughly ground pepper. Stir in the grated cucumber, keeping some back for decoration. Serve the tzatziki and decorate with grated cucumber.

More fresh cream cheese ...

Herb fresh cream cheese

Mix 6 tablespoons (100 g) well drained fresh cream cheese with a pinch salt and 1 tablespoon chopped herbs (chives and parsley).

Fresh cream cheese with seeds

Add a pinch of salt and 1 teaspoon each of sunflower seeds, sesame seeds, and flax seeds to 6 tablespoons (100 g) of very well drained fresh cream cheese. Mix well.

Quark balls

Add 1 pinch of salt to 6 tablespoons (100 g) of well drained full fat quark or fresh cream cheese. Mix and shape into small balls. Roll in 1–2 tablespoons of chopped colorful pepper. Alternatively, roll the balls in chopped chives, garlic, or paprika, or preserve in good-quality oil.

Tip

Put the fresh cream cheese into glass or porcelain storage containers. Seal and chill immediately.

Hearty quark spreads

Quark spreads are quick to make and delicious served with fresh wholewheat bread or jacket potatoes, as a tasty dip at barbecues or with fondues, or as a filling for spicy pancakes and omelets.

I find it easiest to make quark spreads in the food processor using the mixer blade, or in the food chopper if I am making just a small quantity. Important: mix all the other ingredients together first, add the quark at the end, and mix briefly. If you mix for too long, the spread will nearly always become runnier.

Seed spread

Chop 1 tablespoon of pumpkin seeds, sesame seeds, or sunflower seeds. Place in the food processor with 1 cup (250 g) quark, 1 tablespoon pumpkin seed oil or a similar seed oil and salt. Mix well.

Salmon spread

Drain a small can (100 g) of smoked salmon fillets (in oil) and mix in the food processor. Add 1 tablespoon chopped parsley and 1 cup (250 g) quark. Mix together briefly.

Herb spread

Take 1 handful of fresh herbs—for example, parsley, chives, wild marjoram, or dill. Wash, dab dry, and chop coarsely. Place in the food processor with some salt and pepper, mix. Add 1 cup (250 g) quark and mix again briefly. Depending on how soft the spread is, add 1 tablespoon sour cream and/or mineral water.

Tuna spread

Chop up 2 small gherkins. Drain a small can (95 g) of tuna fillets. Mix the tuna in the food processor. Add the gherkins, 1 cup (250 g) quark, and 1 tablespoon chopped parsley mix.

Info

Quark mixed with flaxseed oil is a specialty from the Spreewald region of Germany. In days gone by, this was considered "poor man's food," but today it is prized for its health benefits. This is because flaxseed oil contains many valuable omega-3 fatty acids and, together with quark, provides the body with important nutrients.

TIP

For spreads, I use quark with a higher fat content, which means I can add less fat to the spread. If I am going to add butter or a good-quality special oil such as nut or sesame oil, I use quark with a lower fat content.

Erdäpfelkas

**MAKES APPROX.
1 ¼ CUPS (350 G)**

scant 1 cup (300 g)
very soft steamed
potatoes
3–4 tbsp (45–65 g)
quark (fat content as
required)
1 tbsp sour cream
salt, pepper
1 tbsp chopped
parsley
ground caraway

▓ Leave the potatoes to cool slightly, peel, and press through a potato ricer. Mix the potato purée with the quark and the sour cream and season with salt and pepper. Finally, add the chopped parsley and caraway.

Tip

You can also make Erdäpfelkas using leftover potatoes from the previous day. Just make sure they are the floury kind, so the spread will be creamy.

Liptauer

**MAKES APPROX.
1 ¼ CUPS (300 G)**

½ onion
2 garlic cloves
¼ tsp paprika
salt
1 tbsp butter at
room temperature
1 cup (250 g) quark
(fat cont. as required)
2 tbsp (30 ml) beer
or mineral water (as
required)

Spreads such as Liptauer and the quark recipes on the previous page can be prepared the day before serving. This intensifies the flavor of the herbs and spices, and makes the spread more solid. Store in a small preserving jar, which you can keep for home consumption or give to a host or hostess as a gift.

▓ Peel the onion half and garlic cloves and chop roughly. Place both in a food processor with a mixer blade and chop finely.

▓ Add the paprika, some salt, and the butter. Mix well. Add the quark and mix. Finally, add the beer or mineral water, and mix briefly.

Tip

Why not try adding finely diced red pepper or gherkins to the Liptauer.

The alpine pastures of my childhood —dairy farming then and now

The Pinzgauer is a breed of cattle that was threatened with extinction. It is very tough and due to its undemanding nature is particularly well suited to life in the steep alpine meadows.

My home town of St. Johann im Pongau lies at the entrance to the Großarl valley, the so-called valley of the alpine pastures (it contains about 40 pastures). As my father was an enthusiastic mountaineer, our family spent many hours in the pastures of Großarl and Hüttschlag. The original forms of dairy processing are still practiced in this unique region, and the development of dairy farming is interesting to observe.

What always fascinates me whenever I visit one of the alpine pastures is the deep respect there for the knowledge of previous generations. Local farms produce (raw) milk products that require specific traditional working methods: sour cheeses made from skim milk, all kinds of varieties of butter, and ripened cheese ranging from mild to full flavored—all of which can be enjoyed on the spot as part of a good meal or snack. For those who would like to experience daybreak in an alpine meadow, about 20 pastures in the GrossarItal offer overnight accommodation.

A typical day

The day on the alpine meadows begins with the morning milking. The dairy farmer then usually processes the morning's milk together with the evening milk from the previous day. Throughout the course of the day, the dairy farmers check up on the welfare of the animals. Many alpine meadows are open to visitors, so you might see walkers in the late morning, and dairy farmers welcome guests and visitors throughout the day.
In the evening, the animals are taken back to the stable for milking. Nearly all dairy farmers sell their products on site. In autumn, the cheeses are brought to the farms and marketed there.

Many alpine meadows employ casual staff during the summer months. This gives a rare insight into the world of cheese-making and offers the opportunity to help look after the animals and the guests. But you can also enjoy solitary hours and take some time out. High season varies in the alpine pastures, and can last from June until September, depending on the altitude of the meadow. The weather plays a major role. Early snowfall often forces the dairy farmers to bring their animals into the valley out of the high alps.

Pinzgauer cows rest in front of the Paulhütte inn in the Aigenalm region in Großarl. From here, you can cross the ridge and climb the Kreuzkogel.

Jewels of the alpine gastronomic culture

In the Großarl valley in Austria, as in several other alpine regions, you can find the origins of the region's gastronomic culture. A glimpse into the small dairies inside the alpine meadow chalets shows how sophisticated the cheese culture was in these parts even decades ago. During the summer months, dairy farmers in neighboring meadows would become friends, evenings were and still are often spent together, mutual help went without saying and still does, and experiences and tips are exchanged.

In spite of all the hardship, life in the alpine pastures was and continues to be a sacred, ordered world, in which people lead a simple life far away from all the hustle, bustle, and stress of modern civilization.

Quark, milk, and yeast bread

MAKES 1 LOAF

5 tbsp (70 g) butter
1 cup (250 ml) milk
2 egg yolks
½ cup (125 g) quark
(20% FiDM)
3½ cups (500 g) flour
1 packet dry yeast
½ tsp salt
1 tbsp sugar
flour for the counter
fat for the pan

■ Melt the butter in a pan and add the milk. Then remove the pan from the heat immediately—as the milk should not get too hot. Pour everything into a mixing bowl and stir in the egg yolks and the quark.

■ Mix the flour with the yeast, salt, and sugar. Gradually stir the milk and quark mixture into the flour, and knead until it forms a malleable dough. Cover the mixing bowl and leave the yeast dough in a warm place.

■ Once the volume has doubled, split the dough into three pieces. Roll out each piece into a cord on a floured counter. Weave the cords into a braid and place on a greased baking tray. Cover the yeast braid and leave to rise for a further 20 minutes.

■ Preheat the oven to 350 °F (180 °C) (fan-assisted 320 °F (160 °C)). Bake the yeast braid in the oven for about 40 minutes, remove from the oven, and leave to cool.

Tip

To keep the yeast braid very soft on the outside, turn it over on the baking tray once it has finished baking, and cover with a dish towel.

Puff pastry crescents with quark

MAKES
4 PORTIONS

For the quark puff pastry
1¾ cups (250 g) flour
pinch of salt
1 cup + 2 tbsp
(250 g) cold butter
1 cup (250 g) quark
(20% FiDM)
flour for the counter

Also
fat for frying
confectioners' sugar
for sprinkling

You can also use this puff pastry for strudels, cookies, and cream rolls. The ingredients should all be chilled in advance and the dish should be prepared in the coolest place possible, as the butter can heat up quickly. Then all the ingredients will merge with each other and layers will not form. It is possible to make this quark puff pastry in advance and freeze it.

▓ Place the flour in a mixing bowl, add salt, then break the butter into small pieces and work it into the flour. Rub the quark in until the pastry is firm and comes away from the edge of the bowl without sticking.

▓ Using a rolling pin, roll the pastry out lengthwise on a floured counter and fold it in half twice. Wrap the pastry tile in aluminum foil and chill for about 30 minutes. This procedure is carried out three times in total, so you need to work as quickly as possible.

▓ For the quark crescents, roll the pastry out on a floured counter until it is about ⅕ inch (5 mm) thick. Cut out crescent moons using a cookie cutter. Heat sufficient cooking oil in a large pan and fry the crescents. Sprinkle with confectioners' sugar to serve.

Tip

The consistency of quark can vary greatly—sometimes it is drier, sometimes more watery. If you use homemade quark for the pastry, it is best not to knead in all the flour at once. Instead, hold some back and use it if necessary. It is easy to add flour later on to make pastry that is too sticky firmer, rather than trying to soften pastry that is too stiff. Trust your instinct and the pastry is sure to work!

Apricot dumplings

MAKES
4 PORTIONS

1 cup (250 g) quark
(20% FiDM)
3½ tbsp (50 g) butter
scant 1 cup (130 g)
flour
1 egg
pinch of salt
8 apricots
crumb and sugar
mixture for rolling

You can also use this recipe to make plum or strawberry dumplings. Warm nut butter goes well with the filled dumplings.

▥ In a mixing bowl, knead together the quark, butter, flour, egg, and salt to form a firm dough. Cover the dough and chill for 30 minutes.

▥ In the meantime, wash and dry the apricots. Wrap the apricots one by one in the dough and shape into dumplings. Heat sufficient water in a pan and simmer the dumplings on low heat for about 15 minutes. To serve, roll in the crumb and sugar mixture.

Variation

For **quark semolina dumplings** without a filling, stir together 1 cup (250 g) quark with 1 egg, a pinch of salt, ¼ cup (40 g) semolina, and ⅔ cup (30 g) breadcrumbs. Leave the dough to swell for about 30 minutes, then mold into dumplings. Cook in boiling salted water for a few minutes. Serve with fruit purée or a crumb and hazelnut mixture.

INFO

Apricot dumplings are one of the most well-known Austrian and Bohemian specialties. Austrian dumplings come in various varieties, and with potato, yeast, or quark dough—as in this recipe.

Sweet quark pasta

MAKES
4 PORTIONS

¾ cup + 2 tbsp
(125 g) flour
1 cup (250 g) quark
(20% FiDM)
1 egg
salt
flour for the counter
sugar and cinnamon
crumbs for sprinkling

▦ Knead together the flour, quark, egg, and a pinch of salt to form a dough. Wrap the dough in plastic wrap and chill for about 30 minutes. Then shape the dough into a roll on a floured counter and cut off small pieces.

▦ Bring plenty of salted water to the boil in a pan and cook the quark pasta in it for a few minutes. Serve the quark pasta with a mixture of sugar and cinnamon crumbs or vary with poppy seeds or nuts.

Mom's cheesecake

9 ½ IN (24 CM)
SPRINGFORM
PAN

For the base
1²/₃ cups (250 g)
coarse-grained flour
½ packet baking
powder
5 tbsp (70 g) sugar
9 tbsp (130 g) cold
butter
1 egg
butter & flour for pan
flour for the counter

My mother used to own a guesthouse, and her legendary cheesecake was always on the menu, even though cheesecake was almost completely unknown in our region 40 years ago. We had many guests, including some from Germany, who loved mom's cheesecake.

▓ To make the base, sieve the flour together with the baking powder. Add the sugar, cut the butter into small pieces, and knead it into the flour and sugar mixture together with the egg. Wrap the dough in plastic wrap and chill for about 30 minutes.

▓ Preheat the oven to 340 °F (170 °C). Grease a springform pan and dust with flour. To make the filling, beat the eggs and sugar together in a mixing bowl until light and fluffy. Add the quark. Stir briefly, taking care that the quark does not become too liquid. Add the cream and the custard powder.

▓ Roll the pastry out on a floured counter and place in the pan, leaving a 1 in (3 cm) overhang. Spread the filling over the pastry and cook the cheesecake in the oven for about 50 minutes. After it has cooled, sprinkle with confectioners' sugar.

For the filling
2 eggs
¾ cup + 2 tbsp
(200 g) sugar
2 cups (500 g) quark
(20% FiDM)
2 cups (500 ml)
cream
1 packet custard
powder
confectioners' sugar
for sprinkling

Plum cake

MAKES 1 SHEET
PAN

For the base
1 cup (150 g) coarse-
grained flour
¼ tsp baking powder
pinch of salt
²/₃ cup (150 g) cold
butter
10 tbsp (150 g) quark
(20% FiDM)
butter and flour for
the sheet pan
flour for the counter

For the topping
scant 6 cups (1 kg)
plums
cinnamon and sugar
as required

If the plums are very sour, sprinkle them with sugar before cooking.

▓ Sieve the flour with the baking powder and quickly knead together with a pinch of salt, the butter (chopped into small pieces), and the quark. Wrap the pastry in plastic wrap and chill for about 30 minutes.

▓ Preheat the oven to 350 °C (180 °C). Grease the pan and dust with flour. Wash and core the plums, cut into quarters, and flavor with cinnamon and sugar.

▓ Roll the pastry out on a floured counter and place on the sheet pan. Allow the pastry to overlap the edges and lay the plums on the pastry side by side in a roof tile pattern. Bake the cake in the oven for about 40 minutes.

TIP

This plum cake tastes particularly delicious served with fresh whipped cream.

Quark crumble with cherries

MAKES 1 SHEET PAN

For the base
1 packet baking powder
4 cups (600 g) coarse-grained flour
¾ cup + 2 tbsp (200 g) sugar
1 ¹/₃ cups (300 g) cold butter
1 egg yolk
butter and flour for the sheet pan
flour for the counter

▓ Sieve the baking powder with the flour. Add the sugar, cut the butter into small pieces, and knead it into the flour and sugar mixture together with the egg yolk. Wrap the pastry in plastic wrap and chill for about 30 minutes.

▓ Preheat the oven to 340 °F (170 °C). Grease the sheet pan and dust with flour. To make the filling, stir the quark, sugar, and custard powder together until creamy. Mix the cherries into the quark mixture.

▓ Roll out three-quarters of the pastry on a floured counter and place on the sheet pan. Spread the filling over the pastry. Knead the remaining pastry together with some extra flour and sugar to form crumbs and sprinkle over the filling. Bake the quark crumble in the oven for about 50 minutes.

For the filling
4½ cups (1 kg) quark (20% FiDM)
7 tbsp (100 g) sugar
1 packet custard powder
generous 1lb (500 g) dried cherries (preserved)
flour and sugar for the crumble

Shredded quark pancake

MAKES
4 PORTIONS

1 cup (250 g) quark
(20% FiDM)
1 cup (250 ml) milk
3 eggs
2 tbsp (25–30 g)
sugar
¼ cup + 2 tbsp
(120 g) flour
1 packet custard
powder
fat for frying
confectioners' sugar
for sprinkling

▥ Stir the quark together with the milk, eggs, and sugar until smooth. Then stir in the flour and custard powder. Leave the batter to swell for about 30 minutes.

▥ Heat the cooking oil in a frying pan and pour in the batter. Cook until thick, turning once. When you have finished cooking, cut the pancake into pieces with a spatula. Place the shredded pancake on plates and serve sprinkled with confectioners' sugar.

TIP

It is best to cook the shredded quark pancake in a large frying pan or to make two separate portions.

Quark pancakes

**Makes
4 portions**

For the pancakes
1 cup (250 ml) milk
2 eggs
³/₄ cup + 2 tbsp
(125 g) flour
salt
fat for frying

For the filling
3 eggs
3½ tbsp (50 g) butter
7 tbsp (50 g)
confectioners' sugar
1 heaped tbsp
custard powder
gen. ¾ cup (200 g)
quark (20% FiDM)
fat for the dish

▦ To make the pancakes, stir together the milk, eggs, and flour until smooth. Add salt and leave to swell for about 30 minutes. Heat the cooking oil in a frying pan and cook several thin pancakes one after the other. Leave to cool.

▦ In the meantime, separate the eggs to make the filling. Beat the egg whites until stiff. Mix the butter with the egg yolks and confectioners' sugar until light and fluffy. Add the custard powder and stir the quark in briefly. Then fold in the beaten egg whites.

▦ Preheat the oven to 350 °F (180 °C). Grease an ovenproof dish. Fill the pancakes with the quark mixture, then roll and layer them side by side in the dish. Mix together the cream, eggs, sour cream, and sugar and pour over the pancakes. Bake the pancakes in the oven for about 30 minutes and serve sprinkled with confectioners' sugar.

For the glaze
½ cup (125 ml)
cream
2 eggs
½ cup (125 g) sour
cream
3 tbsp (40 g) sugar
confectioners' sugar
for sprinkling

Quark mousse with raspberries

MAKES
4 PORTIONS

1 cup (250 ml) cream
1 cup (250 g) quark
(20% FiDM)
6 tbsp (100 g)
natural yogurt
1 tbsp sugar (as
required)
1 egg white
3 gelatin leaves
a few nice
raspberries for
decoration

▦ Remove 2 tablespoons of the cream and reserve for the gelatin. Whip the rest of the cream until stiff. Stir the quark together with the yogurt and sugar until light and fluffy. Beat the egg white until stiff.

▦ Soften the gelatin in cold water. Heat the 2 tablespoons of cream in a small pan, squeeze the water from the gelatin, and dissolve in the cream. Stir the gelatin cream into the quark mixture and fold in the whipped cream and beaten egg whites.

▦ Cover the mousse and leave to solidify in the fridge for a few hours, then cut out dumplings. To serve, decorate with the raspberries, and a few raspberry leaves if required.

TIP

You can also spoon the quark mousse into small glasses and serve covered with the raspberries.

Sweet quark creams

... with vanilla

These recipes each make 4 portions. The fat content of the quark is up to you. You could also stir in yogurt or whipped cream.

Use 2 cups (500 ml) milk, 1 packet of custard powder, and 2 tablespoons (25–30 g) sugar. Prepare the custard and leave to cool. Take 1 cup (250 g) quark, stir briefly, stir in the custard, and chill.

... with jam or jelly

Stir together 2 cups (500 g) quark, 2 tablespoons (30 g) yogurt, 2 tablespoons (25–30 g) sugar, and ¼ teaspoon cinnamon. Put ½ tablespoon of jam (apricot, strawberry, or red currant) in the bottom of 4 small glass dishes. Layer the quark cream on top.

... with fruit or flowers and nuts

Whip ½ cup (125 ml) cream until stiff. Stir together 2 cups (500 g) quark, 2 tablespoons (30 g) yogurt, and 2 tablespoons (25–30 g) sugar until smooth. Wash the fruit or edible flowers and cut into small pieces. Fold the cream into the quark cream together with the fruit or flowers and sprinkle with chopped walnuts.

TIP

Quark creams are very popular with children, particularly when served in small dishes. Tasty quark creams with jam, vanilla seeds, and fruit and nuts (from back to front).

Soft cheese—
quick and varied

Soft cheese— an overview

Soft cheeses include Camembert and Brie, red smear cheeses such as Munster and Limburger, and also Feta. Mozzarella and ricotta are quite different types of cheese.

T he most well-known soft cheeses are cheeses with white surface molds such as Camembert and Brie and red smear cheeses such as Romadur and Limburger. Many soft cheeses have to ripen for several weeks and therefore have a much more intense flavor than fresh cheese.

From Normandy and Alsace

There are numerous legends surrounding the discovery of Camembert. However, there is no doubt that the cheese with the white mold originates from France. The variety named Camembert de Normandie has protected designation of origin status in the EU (AOC rating = Appelation d'Origine Contrôlée).

So that the cheese is covered with a fine white bloomy rind when it is finished, the milk is inoculated with special mold fungus cultures before coagulation. During the ripening process, these cultures produce the special flavor and the characteristic appearance. NB: If a soft cheese has a chalky center, this indicates an unripe cheese.

Beneficial mold

The word "mold" can have negative connotations. Nevertheless, the molds used for soft ripened cheeses, washed rind cheeses, and blue cheeses are grown as pure cultures—an example is the prettily named *Penicillium camemberti*. They provide the special flavor and do not present a danger to health. You should take care with foreign or harmful mold, which can be toxic. If you are not sure, it is best to throw the whole cheese away as the mold spores have often penetrated the whole cheese, even when this is not visible.

Bacteria for red smear cheeses

Nearly all red smear soft cheeses come from France too. Some have protected designation of origin status—for example, Munster cheese from Alsace. Nowadays, non-French dairies are also producing red smear soft cheese, such as Limburg from Germany and Romadur from Belgium. The rinds of red smear cheeses can—albeit rarely—be contaminated with listeria, which causes listeriosis. Vulnerable people, such as the elderly, people with reduced immunity, infants, and pregnant women, should be aware of this risk.

Brined curd cheeses

Another type of soft cheese is so-called brined curd cheese, such as Feta, which is made from sheep's milk. Feta has also had protected designation of origin status since the end of 2007, and can be called Feta only if the cheese has been made from sheep's and/or goat's milk, ripened in brine, and produced on the Greek mainland or the island of Lesbos. Therefore, German dairies call their brined curd cheese made from cow's milk either Feta style or Hirtenkäse.

Nutrients in soft cheese

Soft cheese contains key components of milk in concentrated form. Fresh soft cheese contains high quantities of calcium, potassium, and magnesium. Information regarding the nutritional value of homemade products is a guideline only and is subject to deviation depending on the type of milk used and the whey drainage. The fat in soft cheese is easily digestible and provides both fat-soluble vitamins such as Vitamin A and flavor. Soft cheese preserved in oil naturally has a considerably higher fat content, and is very filling.

Popular cheeses made easy

On the following pages, you will find recipes and tips for successful cheese-making at home. Choose from my fresh, unripened soft cheese and popular varieties such as mozzarella, cottage cheese, and ricotta. These cheeses, which can be enjoyed fresh or soft ripened, are all quick to prepare and guarantee the highest quality, provided you use the most natural milk possible. I do not recommend making Camembert or red smear cheeses in your own home unless you have the necessary specialist knowledge.

Fresh soft cheese— here's how

I advise anyone who would like to find out about cheese-making to start off with a simple fresh soft cheese. You can eat this type of cheese either straight away or a few days after making it. This is the best way for you to learn about how milk reacts to different temperatures and the effects of cultures and rennet. This fresh soft cheese is particularly suitable if you do not have a ripening room and prefer a cheese that does not have a very distinctive flavor. You can also make this soft cheese with small quantities of milk.

What type of milk?

The best type of milk for making soft cheese is the most natural milk possible—this could be milk bought from a farm, or fresh, traditionally made milk bought from a store. In my experience, cheese-making using ultra-heat-treated (ESL or UHT) milk does not work. All the same, even if you use non-heat-treated or just pasteurized milk, if the animals have been fed silage then this may affect the coagulation of the milk. Silo feed changes the quality of the milk in such a way that curdling occurs either very slowly or not at all (see page 24).

I have tried all the different types of milk available, including traditionally made fresh milk from a discount store and fresh ESL milk. The fact is, only very few of the types of milk available via retailers are suitable for cheese-making without the addition of ingredients such as calcium chloride. In order to make the product as natural as possible, it is worth using suitable milk. You may want to try making cheese using milk from cows that have been fed with silage. My experience, and that of many of the participants on my courses, is that it is possible. It depends on the composition of the silage.

Ultra-heat-treated milk such as UHT or ESL milk is less suitable for cheese-making. It is best to use natural or traditionally made milk.

More rennet, less starter

Coagulation is different for hard, semihard, and soft cheeses than it is for quark. The milk protein is largely precipitated by rennet, and only partially by lactic acid bacteria. The term "rennet cheese" is therefore used. I even use more rennet (and less buttermilk) for my fresh soft cheese. This speeds up the process and more whey drains away. Three quarts (3 liters) of milk produce about a generous 1¾ cups (450 g) of fresh soft cheese, much less than for quark. I use liquid rennet for soft cheese. Buttermilk is the best culture or starter, in my experience. However, you can also buy special lactic acid cultures.

The correct temperature

The cheese that is produced will vary according to the temperature at which the milk is renneted. I find that milk curdles more quickly when the renneting temperature is toward 95 °F (36 °C)—i.e. higher. If you add the rennet at a lower temperature, this gives the lactic acid bacteria more opportunities to multiply before the rennet has started to work properly.

In general, the curds are only reheated later on in the production of hard cheese. However, I reheat the curds when making certain types of soft cheese, in order to speed up the drainage of the whey. If you cut the coagulum into cubes and begin reheating— this should always be done very carefully, on medium heat—you will see how the whey slowly separates from the curds. The lower the temperature when reheating, the less the whey will drain off and the softer the curds will be. As the temperature rises, an increasing amount of whey will separate from the curds. Once you reach a reheating temperature of 140 °F (60 °C) (as with cottage cheese), a large part of the whey will have drained off. If you raise the temperature any higher, the curds will turn rubbery. Of course, the same principles also apply to other types of cheese-making.

The consistency of the cheese will change several times, depending on how long you leave the whey to drain off. Whey drains off considerably faster from curds that have been reheated than from curds that have not been reheated or have been only slightly reheated.

Cheese molds for soft cheese

Scoop the remaining curds and whey mixture into cheese molds. If you are making cheese for your own consumption, you can use food-grade molds made of plastic or wood. These give the cheese the desired shape and let additional whey drain off.

It is best to buy cheese molds that are made of food-grade materials. The cheese molds should have drainage holes on all sides and small feet at the bottom, so that the whey can drain away easily. If the molds do not have feet at the bottom, you can simply rest them on two pieces of wood. If it is your first attempt at making soft cheese, a sieve will work well.

There is a wide range of cheese molds available from suppliers. To make a scant 1¼ cups (300 g) of soft cheese from 2 quarts (2 liters) of milk, you will need a rectangular cheese mold 6 x 2½ x 2¾ inches (15 x 6 x 7 cm). If you split the same amount into 2 molds of this size, the whey will drain away more quickly.

Standard commercial molds are made from food-grade plastic as lactic acid attacks normal plastic. Heart-shape or round cheese molds are suitable if you want to serve the soft cheese whole or give it as a gift.

A wide range of food-grade molds is available from suppliers.

Mistakes in cheese-making

Unlike quark, fresh soft cheese is relatively unprotected against harmful bacteria and microbes by its own lactic acid bacteria. This means it is easy to end up with a defective product. If, for example, your cheese swells or has a strange taste, you should throw it away immediately. When making your own dairy products, always pay attention to possible sources of error. Is the rennet still fresh? Are you boiling your equipment from time to time, to ensure unwanted bacteria cannot multiply? And if you are using your own milk, has the animal feed changed? Are the animals being fed with silage—for example, in cooler seasons (see page 24)?

Fresh soft cheese in the kitchen

Homemade fresh soft cheese is a high-quality, low-cost alternative to store-bought cheese. Fresh soft cheese should be used and processed quickly. If you store it in the fridge for a few days, it is best to use a sealed container, or to preserve the cheese in brine or oil.

Fresh soft cheese can be added to pasta dishes and bakes, as well as to all kinds of pizza variation. You can also use soft cheese preserved in oil as a cheese topping. For a delicious salad ingredient, try preserving your soft cheese in a special oil.

Fresh homemade soft cheese

MAKES SCANT
1 ¼ CUPS
(300 G)
APPROX.

2 quarts (2 liters) full-
fat milk
2 tbsp (30 ml)
buttermilk (or
corresponding
amount of culture)
rennet (amount for
cheese according to
the instructions on
the packet)

For my fresh soft cheese, I use buttermilk as a starter (or culture), and add more rennet than I would for making quark. In just a few hours' time, I have a pleasant, mild cheese that is also stable and firm.

▓ In a large pan, heat the milk to 95 °F (36 °C) (use a thermometer), add the buttermilk or culture, and stir well. Then mix the rennet with some water and mix into the milk mixture using a whisk. Finally, bring the milk to a standstill with a counter movement of the whisk.

▓ After 30 to 60 minutes, once the milk has formed a coagulum, cut it lengthwise and crosswise (ideally with a cheese harp). Leave the curds to one side for about 30 minutes.

▓ If you want to, you can reheat the curds to 107 °F (42 °C) before leaving them to one side for 30 minutes. (I like making cheese according to this variation with reheating, although soft cheese is not really reheated. However, it can take a long time for the whey to drain if you do not reheat the curds, and soft cheese curds that are not reheated easily absorb kitchen smells.)

▓ Skim the curds into prepared cheese molds and leave the whey to drain off for about 4 to 8 hours (2 to 4 hours for the reheated variation).

For optimal whey drainage, you can also turn the cheese after a while. Pour warm whey over the cheese from time to time. This will keep the pores of the cheese grains open and leave the whey to drain away easily from inside. Otherwise there is the danger that the outer pores will close when there is still whey inside the cheese, which can cause abnormal fermentation (swelling). This is a particular risk in very dry rooms (the result of heating in winter).

Variations

▓ If you prefer **spicy soft cheese**, you can add salt or pepper to the curds after you have placed them in the cheese mold (no stirring!). I recommend high-quality natural salt, herb salt, or ground pepper.

▓ Or you can preserve the **soft cheese in brine**. To fill a 17 ounce (500 ml) preserving jar, boil 1½ cups (350 ml) water with 3 teaspoons (15–18 g) salt until the salt has dissolved. Leave the salt water to cool (if you are in a hurry, put the salt water in a container in the freezer). Cut 1¼ cups (300 g) fresh soft cheese into pieces and place in the preserving jar. Add the salt water, seal the jar, and place in the refrigerator.

TIP

Use the highest quality salt possible for the brine. This really adds to the taste of soft cheese. I prefer to use hand-harvested sea salt.

Soft cheese with prunes

MAKES
4 PORTIONS

10 prunes
6 tbsp (100 g) fresh,
salted soft cheese
7 tbsp (100 ml)
sesame oil

My fresh soft cheese is perfect for preserving. It naturally has a very mild taste and therefore absorbs the flavor of the preserving oil and the seasoning within 1 to 2 days.

▥ Core the prunes and cut into small pieces. Cut the soft cheese into cubes. Add the soft cheese and prunes alternately to a 9 ounce (250 ml) preserving jar, and top up with the sesame oil.

Tip

Soft cheese with prunes makes a very good salad ingredient. Wash some seasonal lettuce and cut into bite-size pieces. Wash 5 cocktail tomatoes, cut into quarters, and add to the lettuce. Season everything with balsamic vinegar, salt, and ½ tablespoon chopped herbs. Add 6 tablespoons (100 g) soft cheese with prunes.

Preserved soft cheese

... with walnuts

Chop 6 tablespoons (100 g) fresh soft cheese into small cubes and mix well with ½ teaspoon salt. Chop 1 tablespoon (7 g) walnuts roughly and layer in the preserving jar, alternating with the soft cheese. Finally, add 1 teaspoon honey, followed by ½ cup (120 ml) walnut oil. Ensure everything is well covered.

INFO

All recipes for preserving soft cheese are for one 9 ounce (250 ml) preserving jar (with lid).

... in truffle oil

Chop 6 tablespoons (100 g) fresh soft cheese into small cubes and layer in the preserving jar together with 1 teaspoon cloves. Top up with ½ cup (120 ml) truffle oil.

... with dried tomatoes

Chop 6 tablespoons (100 g) fresh soft cheese into small cubes and layer in the preserving jar, alternating with 2 tablespoons finely sliced, dried tomatoes. Top up with 7 tablespoons (100 ml) cold-pressed olive oil.

Soft cheese in vine leaves

MAKES
4 PORTIONS

4 vine leaves (fresh
or bought)
generous ¾ cup
(200 g) fresh soft
cheese
2 cocktail tomatoes

▨ Blanch the vine leaves in boiling water for a few minutes, or use bought vine leaves. Cut the soft cheese into four pieces. Wash and quarter the cocktail tomatoes.

▨ Place a piece of cheese and 2 cocktail tomato quarters on each vine leaf. To serve, roll up the vine leaf, tucking one end in slightly.

Tip

Camembert and Feta also taste very good in vine leaves.

Soft cheese platter

MAKES APPROX.
4 PORTIONS

6 tbsp (100 g) fresh
soft cheese
3½ oz (100 g) Brie
8 small roses
wholewheat bread

If you prepare the cheese platter a few hours before serving, the soft cheese will absorb the taste of the Brie slightly. As a variation, you could use any other type of mold-ripened cheese.

▨ Cut both the fresh soft cheese and the Brie into eight long pieces. Place the pieces of cheese side by side on the platter. Decorate with small roses and serve with wholewheat bread.

Variation

To make **soft cheese brochettes** (see page 116, right-hand side), take 4 cocktail sticks and place 2 cubes of different soft cheese (each approx. ½ ounce / 15 g), one grape, and some wild marjoram on each stick. Place the brochettes on lemon balm leaves.

Tip

Soft cheese also tastes good on toasted ciabatta with fresh figs and arugula or another spicy salad vegetable.

Obatzda

MAKES APPROX.
¾ CUP (200 G)

½ onion
3½ tbsp (50 g) soft
butter
3½ tbsp (50 g) soft
cheese
1¾ oz (50 g)
Camembert
1¾ oz (50 g) Brie
¼ tsp sweet paprika
salt (as required)

This Bavarian cheese spread is a good use for leftover soft cheese. It is easy to make and very tasty.

▧ The easiest way to make Obatzda is in a food processor, using the mixer blade. First, peel the onion half and chop finely in the mixer. Add the soft butter and mix until light and fluffy.

▧ Then add the soft cheese, Camembert, and Brie. Mix again. Season the spread with paprika and salt as required. Serve with fresh wholewheat bread.

Tip

You can decorate the Obatzda with freshly chopped chives.

Baked Camembert

MAKES
4 PORTIONS

generous 1 ½ cups
(400 g) Camembert,
cut into ½ inch
(1.5 cm) pieces
1 egg
flour and bread-
crumbs for the
coating
oil for frying
grapes

▓ Cut the Camembert into ½ inch (1.5 cm) pieces. Whisk the egg in a deep dish. Place some flour and breadcrumbs in 2 other deep dishes. First roll the Camembert pieces in the flour, then dip in the whisked egg, then roll in the crumbs.

▓ Heat sufficient oil in a frying pan. Fry the crumb-coated Camembert pieces in the hot oil until golden brown. Wash the grapes, dab dry, and serve with the baked Camembert.

TIP

Camembert is not the only soft cheese suitable for coating with crumbs. You can also try soft cheese, Feta, and mozzarella.

Whey for health and beauty

Whey separates from curds when the coagulum is cut. It tastes very good in drinks—for example, in this apple and mango purée with whey.

In the past, whey was considered nothing more than a byproduct of cheese-making, and was often simply fed to animals or scattered over the fields. It is only in recent decades that people have remembered that whey contains high-quality and easily digestible protein. Whey proteins are even thought to strengthen the immune system. In addition, whey provides iodine, calcium, potassium, magnesium, and B vitamins and is practically fat free. Last but not least, the high milk sugar (lactose) content of whey means that people have for a long time used it to boost digestion. It is therefore not surprising that whey cures were still recommended until relatively recently.

Sweet whey and sour whey

The type of whey produced will differ depending on whether the milk protein has been converted into lactic acid by rennet or starter bacteria. If the milk was curdled with lactic acid bacteria (fresh cheese, sour milk cheese), this will produce sour whey. If, however, the milk was curdled following the addition of rennet (soft, semihard and hard cheese), this is known as sweet coagulation, and the result is sweet whey or rennet whey. Nowadays, whey is once again a popular drink. It is added to whey-based products and is the basic product for whey powder. Whey has wide application in the food and cosmetics industries. It is also an excellent substitute for water in the production of yeast dough. Sour whey is used in bread-making.

Cheese from whey

Whey contains a relatively high amount of protein and can therefore be made into cheese itself—a completely different type of cheese called whey cheese or whey protein cheese. There are two ways to make this cheese.

You can mix (sweet) whey with milk or cream and boil it down to a thick brownish mass, which can then be left to solidify in a mold. This so-called **brunost** is particularly common in Scandinavia (*mysost*, *geitost*, etc.) and is often also produced from goat's whey.

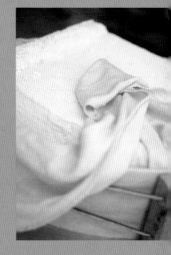

Or you can reheat and reacidify the whey, allow the whey proteins to coagulate, and use the resulting product like fresh cheese. Such **whey cheeses** are common in southern Europe—Italian ricotta and Greek manouri are both made in this way.

Homemade ricotta

MAKES APPROX.
1 ⅓ CUPS (350 G)

1 quart (1 liter) buttermilk
2 quarts (2 liters) full-fat milk
salt (as required)

Below is a very simple recipe for making ricotta from milk and buttermilk.

■ Add the buttermilk to the milk, stir well, and bring to the boil. To begin with, scrape the base of the pan continually with a spatula, to ensure the milk mixture does not burn onto the pan. Then bring the milk mixture to the boil and cook for a few minutes, allowing the whey to separate from the coagulated protein.

■ Scoop the curds into a cheesecloth placed inside a sieve. If you would like to salt your cheese, add a pinch of salt now.

■ Move the cheesecloth back and forth, letting the whey run off. As soon as the desired consistency has been reached, place the cheese in china bowls with lids and chill.

Tip

Ricotta goes well with pasta—either in a sauce with spinach or tomatoes or as a filling for cannelloni. However, sweet pancakes are also delicious filled with ricotta-based creams.

Homemade cottage cheese

Cottage cheese and fresh cheese are among the most popular types of cheese. They are easy to make and taste great even on their own.

MAKES APPROX.
¾ CUP (200 G)

1 quart (1 liter) full-fat milk
1 tbsp (15 ml) buttermilk
rennet (amount for cheese according to the instructions on the packet)
salt
6 tbsp (100 g) sour cream

Cottage cheese is also called "granular fresh cheese" and comes from the UK and the USA. Because it requires more rennet than buttermilk to curdle, I classify it as a soft cheese.

▦ Place the milk in a pan and heat to 95 °F (36 °C) (use a thermometer). Add the buttermilk and stir well. Then mix the rennet with some water and stir into the milk mixture using a whisk (the milk mixture should still be 90 °F (32 °C), heat if necessary). Finally, bring the milk to a standstill with a counter movement of the whisk.

▦ After 30 to 45 minutes, when the milk has formed a coagulum, cut it lengthwise and crosswise (ideally with a cheese harp). Then heat the milk to 140 °F (60 °C) while stirring. The whey will separate from the curds and the curds will take on a light, rubbery consistency.

▦ Ladle the curds into a sieve and wash under very cold running water. Rub the curds between your fingers until small curd granules form.

▦ Salt the curd granules and mix with the sour cream. Place the finished cottage cheese in a sealable container and store in the refrigerator.

TIP

Cottage cheese is delicious served with jacked potatoes or wholewheat bread. It also goes well with herbs, radishes, and berries.

Popular cheese from Italy

Mozzarella is a bit more challenging to make, but you are rewarded with a very tasty product at the end. It is not really a soft cheese, but is part of the special group of Italian curd cheeses called "pasta filata" (*formaggi a pasta filata*—cheese from stretched dough). The curds are steeped in very hot whey or water and then kneaded until the characteristic stringy texture is obtained.

The cheese is usually shaped into round balls and placed in brine. In Italy, there are also other shapes. Bocconcini are small balls (mini mozzarella), and treccia is a braid made from three mozzarella strands. Mozzarella was first made in Italy near Naples from the milk of water buffalos, however the version from cow's milk is more common in Austria—in Italian this is *fior di latte*.

Mozzarella contains about 60% water, depending on the fat content, and this is another reason why it fits well in the soft cheese group. Another *pasta filata* cheese type is provolone, which is ripened and sometimes smoked.

Homemade mozzarella

Makes approx.
¾ cup (200 g)

2 quarts (2 liters) full-fat milk
1 tbsp (15 ml) buttermilk
rennet (amount for cheese according to the instructions on the packet)

Because mozzarella is quite laborious to make with all the pulling and kneading required, and demands a lot of practice, I have modified the method. It works well with small quantities for home consumption.

▥ Place the milk in a large pan and heat to 95 °F (36 °C) (use a thermometer). Add the buttermilk and stir well. Then mix the rennet with some water and stir into the milk mixture using a whisk. Finally, bring the milk to a standstill with a counter movement of the whisk.

▥ After 30 minutes, when the milk has formed a coagulum, cut it lengthwise and crosswise (ideally with a cheese harp).

▥ Leave the curds to one side for 30 minutes, so the curds can separate and the whey can drain off.

▥ Scoop the curds carefully into a cheesecloth placed inside a sieve. Move the cheesecloth back and forth from time to time, leaving the whey to run off (see the top picture above).

▓ Then place the curds and the cloth on a flat grill (e.g. the grill of a food dehydrator). This will speed up whey drainage. In the meantime, heat the whey (or water) that has run off, separate the curds into three portions, and lower each portion into the boiling whey using a flat ladle with holes. Cook for 1 minute, then remove.

▓ Take small pieces of the curd, place them in a cloth, and roll them into mozzarella balls of the size you require. If you are more experienced, you can shape the mozzarella balls without a cloth (see the lower picture on page 136).

▓ Place the balls in jars and cover with brine. To make the brine, stir in 1 teaspoon salt per 7 tablespoons (100 ml) of water. Boil until the salt has dissolved, then leave to cool.

Feta—ripening in brine

Brined curd cheese such as feta ripens directly in brine. The drained cheese mass is cut into cubes of about 2 pounds (1 kg) and submerged in a solution of whey and brine in airtight barrels or vessels, where it ripens over the course of 45 to 60 days. The brine makes feta relatively salty. If you would like to reduce the salt content before eating, you can place the feta in water before serving. Incidentally, "feta" is Greek for "slice," and refers to the traditional serving method.

Feta-style soft cheese

MAKES APPROX.
1 ¼ CUPS (300 G)

2 quarts (2 liters) full-fat milk
3 tbsp (45 ml) buttermilk
rennet (amount for cheese according to the instructions on the packet)

▦ Place the milk in a large pan and heat to 95 °F (36 °C) (use a thermometer). Add the buttermilk and stir well. Then mix the rennet with some water and stir into the milk mixture using a whisk (the milk mixture should still be 90 °F (32 °C), heat if necessary). Finally, bring the milk to a standstill with a counter movement of the whisk.

▦ After 30 to 60 minutes, once the milk has formed a coagulum, cut it lengthwise and crosswise (ideally with a cheese harp).

▦ Then heat the milk to 107 °F (42 °C) and agitate the coagulum with the whisk for about 10 minutes, until the curds are roughly hazelnut size. Leave the curds in the whey for 30 minutes or so.

▦ Then scoop the curds into a cheese mold, salt, and leave to drain. Once the whey has drained away, cut the cheese into slices.

A delicious cheese for Greek-style salads! You can enjoy the cheese straight away or store in the refrigerator in a sealed container filled with brine solution (1 teaspoon salt per 7 tablespoons (100 ml) of water).

INFO

This type of cheese is similar to Feta, but I have modified the cooking method so it is easy to make at home.

Good things take time
—semihard and
hard cheese

Aged cheese

To complete our look at the large family of cheeses, we shall consider semihard and hard aged cheeses. In the previous two chapters, we have become almost fully immersed in the world of cheese-making. We know about different lactic acid bacteria and renneting times, and about reheating curds. We can build on these fundamentals as we continue to learn about cheese.

Regional specialties

Because different families of cheese require different storage conditions, this has led to the development of regional cheese centers. Take, for example, Appenzeller cheese from the Appenzell region of Switzerland, Tilsiter cheese from the Russian town formerly known as Tilsit, and Edam from the town of Edam in the Netherlands. All such cheese types point to a region or a town in which they have been and continue to be produced in the traditional way. Cheese-makers in these places developed special procedures for production, but also for ripening. Rooms were set up—usually in cellars—that offered optimum ripening conditions. Even today, regionality and ripening quality determine the characteristics of thousands of types of cheese.

Hard cheese—with and without holes

Well-known hard cheeses include Bergkäse, Emmentaler, cheddar, Parmesan, and Manchego. They are all relatively solid, because the curd is mixed for a long time and broken up into small pieces during the cheese-making process. Moreover, hard cheeses usually ripen for a long time (up to 3 years), so they contain a lot of dry mass (at least 60%). In general, the longer a cheese ripens, the more intense its flavor. The low water content means that hard cheese lasts for a very long time.

Some cheese types will naturally develop holes during the ripening process. As the ripening time increases, specific lactic acid bacteria break down an increasing amount of lactose or lactic acid into gaseous carbon dioxide, which forms holes in the cheese. The size of the holes will vary depending on the type and amount of lactic acid bacteria added. For example, Emmentaler has large holes, while Bergkäse and Gruyère have smaller holes.

During cheese ripening, the carbohydrate, protein, and fat components of the cheese undergo chemical and enzymatic transformation.

Semihard cheese—semisolid, solid, with mold

Semihard cheeses include Gouda, Edam, Tilsiter, Leerdamer, cheddar, Fontina, Appenzeller, raclette, and Höhlenkäse. With a dry mass content of 50 to 60%, these cheeses are a bit softer than hard cheese and can easily be cut into thin slices. Semisolid, semihard cheeses such as Butterkäse, Gorgonzola, Roquefort, Blue Stilton, Reblochon, Fol Epi, Bel Paese, and Esrom are even softer and more malleable and have a dry mass of

just 45 to 60%. Both semihard cheese types take much less time to ripen and will keep for a maximum of ten days.

When making **edible mold cheeses** such as Gorgonzola, Stilton, or Roquefort, the milk is inoculated with specific mold fungus cultures before cheese-making. During the ripening period, these cultures develop and produce the characteristic flavor and appearance. However, in the case of cheeses such as Camembert, the mold only grows on the outside. With Gorgonzola the mold goes right through the cheese. This is achieved by inserting fine needles into the cheese during the aging process, creating channels that allow the mold to grow.

Raw milk cheese

In some countries, specific types of cheese are also available in raw milk variations, using milk from cows, sheep, or goats. To produce this type of cheese, the untreated milk (raw milk) should not be heated above 104 °F (40 °C), and specific hygiene regulations need to be observed. Because of the low temperature, fewer microbes are killed off, and a range of bacteria are present. These produce the popular, intense flavor. If you eat raw milk cheese, you can be sure the cheese is of a high quality. This is because only milk from specially fed animals can be made into cheese without being heat treated. Harmful microbes can also survive in raw milk cheese, which is why pregnant and breastfeeding women, infants, the elderly, and people with a weak immune system are advised not to eat it. Raw milk cheese should always be clearly labeled ("made with raw milk" / *au lait cru*). Hard cheeses such as Appenzeller, Emmentaler, and Bergkäse are the only exception to this rule. For example, you can assume that Allgäuer Emmentaler and Allgäuer Bergkäse are always made from raw milk. If in doubt, ask at your local cheese shop.

Small dairies and alpine pastures

France is known for its wide variety of cheeses. It produces over 1000 different types, from soft cheeses to edible mold varieties and thoroughbred hard cheeses.

A lot has changed in cheese production. You will seldom find raw milk cheeses on offer in the supermarket. While ripening in cellars is welcome, cheese is expected to stay unchanged for as long as possible in the store. This has a detrimental effect on the taste. A true cheese-lover will try to buy creative cheese variations in small dairies, but will also buy good-quality products from retailers.

In my part of the world, there is a long tradition of cheese-making in the alpine pastures in the summer months, and no cheese is like any other. Each type has its individual flavor and smell. Cheese is made with very simple resources and equipment. In general, the cheese is made from raw milk, and only in very small quantities. Old, traditional knowledge is handed down from one generation to the next. People tend to work by instinct, and very few recipes have been written down and passed on. Cheese-making is learned by joining in with the various processes.

If you wander through our beautiful alpine regions, you can watch many cheese-makers at work, and then enjoy a cheese platter outside the chalet. And you will discover a rich variety of naturally produced cheeses.

The long road to aged cheese

At first glance, it appears very easy to make semihard and hard cheese, but it requires instinct, the right ripening environment, and lots of time to make a tasty ripened cheese out of fresh cheese. After the milk has curdled, the curds have been cut, and the whey has drained away, semihard and hard cheeses still need to be pressed, bathed, and ripened.

The final consistency of the cheese is dependent on several factors. Some cheeses are reheated after coagulation in order to separate more whey. The higher the temperature, the more solid the consistency of the cheese later on, and the higher its dry mass content. But the addition of cream also plays a role. Cheeses that contain cream are generally softer.

Cheese pressing

A significant factor for the consistency of the final cheese is the pressing. This involves pressing the curds with weights, after they have been scooped into molds and some whey has drained off (approx. ½–1 hour). Start with a low press weight, so the cheese stays permeable on the outside and the whey can drain out easily. If the press weight is too heavy at the beginning, the outer pores will become blocked, whey will collect inside the cheese, and this can lead to ripening defects (swollen cheese).

During the pressing procedure, the cheese should not be allowed to cool down too much, to ensure the lactic acid bacteria can work optimally.

Pressing takes place at normal room temperature. I have made my own press weights by filling several jars with different amounts of sandblasting grains. If you are making small amounts of cheese, you could use books, or bags of flour or salt, for pressing. You could buy a cheese press suitable for producing small quantities of cheese.

In my experience, cheeses that have been reheated at a higher temperature need less time for pressing. The softer the cheese, the lower the weight you will need to start with. With very flat cheeses just 2 inches (5 cm) high, I begin with a press weight of 2 pounds (1 kg) for 1 hour, then turn the cheese and press for another hour. I then double the press weight to 4 ¼ pounds (2 kg) and press for 2 hours, before turning the cheese and pressing for another 2 hours.

Salt baths and ripening

The cheese mass will take between 1 hour and several days to become stable in the mold, depending on the type of cheese. The young cheese loaf is then placed in a salt bath (15–22% salt content), which also draws out whey and encourages the development of a nice cheese rind. The longer the cheese is left in the salt bath, the larger, harder, and saltier it will be later on.

After the salt bath, the cheese loaf is ready to be stored in special ripening rooms. The cheese is examined at regular intervals during this period. Storage also makes the cheese drier and therefore harder. The physical conditions in the ripening room and climatic conditions determine the flavor of the cheese and give it its unique features. Cheese can take between several months and a few years to ripen. The softer the consistency of the cheese, the shorter the ripening period. For example, Camembert needs 1–2 weeks to mature, Romadur needs 2–4 weeks, and Emmental needs 3–10 months. Very hard cheese such as Parmesan can age for up to 36 months.

The ripening room—a decisive factor

The biggest challenge for ripening cheese is finding a suitable ripening room. The room should be as free from foreign smells and microbes as possible, but also contain as many beneficial bacteria as possible.

Ripening rooms need very high air humidity of up to 90%. Ripening usually takes place on wood, which also affects the flavor of the cheese. During ripening, the cheeses are turned, then wiped by hand. They are possibly rubbed with salt, wine, herbs or ash, and inspected regularly. Red smear cheeses are regularly brushed, smeared, or sprayed with red culture.

Optimum ripening conditions usually develop over the course of time, so that ripening may be delayed in very new cheese rooms. In the alpine pastures, for example, the ripening rooms are used only during the summer months. Here, the cheeses take longer to ripen in the spring than at the end of the season, when cheeses have been stored for a long time and a suitable ripening climate has developed.

Some semihard cheeses are coated with wax before ripening. The wax coating provides protection against contamination, water, and light. However, the cheese will ripen more slowly and have a milder flavor.

Semihard and hard cheese in the kitchen

Because this book deals with making cheese at home, I would not really recommend making aged cheese, as ideally this requires an appropriate ripening room. All the same, I would like to introduce you to the world of aged cheeses, even if we limit ourselves to a few failsafe basic recipes, none of which requires a long ripening period.

Aging cheese at home

Modern homes rarely possess ideal ripening conditions as far as temperature and air humidity are concerned. If you live in an older house, you may have a cellar (in Europe sometimes called an earth cellar), which is optimally suited for cheese ripening provided it is mold free. However, I would not recommend ripening cheese next to other foodstuffs.

A separate storage room for cheese is only worth having if you make enough cheese. However, you could experiment with using a "ripening box." Remember that ripening cheese can have a very intense smell. I have a mini hothouse that I use for ripening my cheeses as unfortunately our cellar is not suitable. A mini hothouse or a ripening box is a good option for cheeses that are 1–2 inches (3–5 cm) high, as these mature quickly.

How to store cheese properly

To store cheese in the refrigerator, first wrap it in paper, and then place it inside a larger plastic container. Some people recommend just using paper to store mature cheese in the refrigerator, but I would not advise this because of the very intense smell. You can also place a dish towel or a few pieces of kitchen roll inside the plastic container. This will help to keep the cheese fresh and prevent it from "sweating." The best place is the vegetable drawer. Feta and cheeses in brine as well as mozzarella should be stored in airtight jars.

Making a cheese platter

Cheese should be removed from the refrigerator approximately 30 minutes before consumption, to let it develop its full flavor. Although it is practical to arrange different types of cheese on one plate, you might want to put each type of cheese on a separate plate, in order to maintain the individual flavors. Garnish strong, pungent cheeses with grapes or Feta. For mozzarella try tomatoes, and for fresh cheeses use aromatic herbs. Fresh vine leaves and flowers such as nasturtiums, roses, and borage are also good for decoration. I think it is good to present special types of cheese whole on wooden boards, so that guests can cut their favorites themselves.

Suggested wine and beer pairings

Make sure the cheese platter contains a selection of soft, semihard, and hard cheeses with different flavors.

Make sure the drinks harmonize with the types of cheese on offer. Mild, dry wine goes well with mild cheese. For a cheese buffet with very fresh cheeses and spreads, you can also serve sparkling wine—perfect on balmy summer evenings! For very mature cheeses, fruity red wine is a good option. The type of wine should always be determined by the flavor of the most mature cheese. If you are serving beer, try light varieties with mild or fresh cheese, and stronger beers with very mature cheese.

A note on lactose in hard cheese

Here is a note for people who are lactose intolerant. Most of the milk sugar (lactose) is drained from the curds with the whey. The remaining lactose is processed by the lactic acid bacteria during ripening. Very mature cheese therefore contains hardly any lactose—it is effectively lactose free.

Visiting the cheese sommelier

Sommeliers (wine stewards) are employed in the wine trade and in fine restaurants, where they provide expert advice to guests and the restaurant owner. In restaurants, the sommelier advises guests on suitable wines to go with their meal. The sommelier is also responsible for wine procurement, wine storage, and wine cellar rotation.

The wine sommelier has been about for a long time, but the cheese sommelier is a relatively new concept. All the same, cheese sommeliers are becoming more common, with training offered by some large organizations.

How to assess cheese properly

To assess the quality of a cheese, a cheese sommelier must know about cheese production and the reasons for things that may go wrong, as well as about the sensory fundamentals. Hygiene deficiencies in milk production and cheese-making may lead to a range of problems in cheese ripening. The sommelier should also know about so-called affinage, the art of cheese aging and maturing—including treating with wine, stock, or brine.

Like the wine sommelier, the cheese sommelier has recourse to a specialist vocabulary to help in the sensory assessment of types of cheese. Cheeses may be classified as sandy, nutty or winy, earthy or glazed, and fatty or musty. Knowledge of cutting techniques and good cheese combinations complete the cheese sommelier's specialist knowledge, making this food industry expert invaluable in advising diners and customers at specialist cheese stores.

Cheese platter

SERVES
APPROX. 6

10 tbsp (150 g)
Emmental
1 round (150 g)
Camembert
5½ oz (150 g)
Bergkäse
2½ cups (500 g)
grapes
1²/₃ cups (250 g)
cherry tomatoes

■ Arrange all ingredients decoratively, in different size pieces. If required, place in the fridge and remove about 15 minutes before consumption.

■ The main garnishes for cheese are nuts, pumpkin seeds, and grapes. Sour vegetables, citrus fruits, pepper, and paprika go less well with cheese.

Homemade semihard cheese

We will now talk about making aged cheeses. The nature of the finished cheese will be dependent on the reheating temperature, the size of the curds, the skimming of whey, and the addition of water during the reheating process. Sheep's and goat's milk are also very suitable for semihard cheeses.

Semihard cheese

MAKES APPROX.
7 OZ (200 G)

2 quarts (2 liters) full-fat milk
2 tbsp (30 ml) buttermilk (or corresponding amount of culture)
rennet (according to the instructions on the packet)
10 tbsp (200 g) salt

▥ Place the milk in a large pan and heat to 93 °F (34 °C) (use a thermometer). Add the buttermilk or culture and stir well. Leave the mixture to stand at room temperature for about 30 minutes.

▥ Mix the rennet with some water and stir into the milk mixture using a whisk. Finally, bring the milk to a standstill with a counter movement of the whisk.

▥ After 30 to 60 minutes, the milk will form a coagulum. Insert a knife into the coagulum, and if the curds split along a clean line and are not too soft or milky, and the whey separates, it is the right time to cut the curds. Then cut across the coagulum or the curds lengthwise and widthwise and agitate the coagulum until almond-size curds are formed. Leave to stand for about 30 minutes.

▥ Reheat the curds to 104 °F (40 °C) while stirring, then leave to one side for a further 30 minutes. Important: while stirring, keep measuring the temperature of the curds with a thermometer to ensure the temperature is constant throughout. Then leave the curds to one side again for 30 minutes. Scoop into prepared cheese molds. Allow the whey to drain off for 30 minutes, then turn the cheese and drain it for a further 30 minutes.

▥ To begin, press with a weight of 2 pounds (1 kg) for 1 hour. Turn the cheese and press for another hour. Then press with 4¼ pounds (2 kg) for 2 hours, turn the cheese, and press for another 2 hours. If the optimum amount of whey has drained off, the cheese will feel firm and resistant to the touch. Otherwise press again, until the whey has drained off fully.

For the brine, add 10 tablespoons (200 g) salt to 1 quart (1 liter) of water. Stir the salt in well. Soak the cheese in the brine for 1 to 2 hours (depending on the thickness—for cheeses of ¾–1 inch (2–3 cm) high for 1 hour, otherwise 1 hour longer per 1 inch (3 cm). Finally, dry the cheese and place in the ripening room, ripening box, or a mini hothouse.

Info

At home, the press weight and the pressing time are not always constant. All kinds of factors can affect the consistency of the cheese, therefore consider these instructions as just guidelines. The pressing time may be shorter if the whey drains off well. Rely on observing the drainage of the whey and on the touch test, which you should carry out after each pressing procedure. The only thing that is important is to start with a low weight, so the edges do not become blocked.

The Munster valley in Alsace, France, produces many varieties of farmhouse cheese. They are typically eaten with the rind, and sometimes also with caraway.

Semihard washed-curd cheese

MAKES APPROX.
7 OZ (200 G)

2 quarts (2 liters) full-
fat milk
2 tbsp (30 ml)
buttermilk (or
corresponding
amount of culture)
rennet (according to
the instructions on
the packet)
½ tsp salt
salt for rubbing

This recipe produces two cheeses about ¾ inch (2 cm) high. The advantage of this size is shorter whey drainage, salt bath, and ripening times. If you are experienced at cheese-making, you can double the amount of milk, along with the press weight, salt bath, and ripening times.

▨ Place the milk in a pan and heat to 95 °F (36 °C) (use a thermometer). Add the buttermilk or culture and stir well, leave to stand for 30 minutes. Add the rennet and water mixture, stir well. Finally, bring the milk to a standstill with a counter movement of the whisk.

▨ After 30 to 60 minutes, the milk will form a coagulum. Cut across the coagulum lengthwise and widthwise. Then agitate the coagulum carefully until almond-size curds are formed.

▨ Leave the curds to one side for about 30 minutes. Skim off 1 quart (1 liter) of whey and replace this whey with water at 120 °F (50 °C). Heat everything to 107 °F (42 °C) again and stir in one direction for 5 minutes, then leave the curds to stand for another 30 minutes.

▨ Scoop the curds into two prepared molds. Add ½ teaspoon salt and leave the whey to drain. This will take about 1 hour. Turn the cheese so that the whey can drain away easily again. This will take about 1 hour.

▨ Then press the cheese for 1 hour with a weight of 2 pounds (1 kg). Turn and repeat the process. Then press again for 1 hour with 4¼ pounds (2 kg), turn and repeat the process. The whey should be almost completely gone by this time, otherwise press again, until the cheese is firm and resistant to the touch.

▨ Rub salt into the cheese. Finally, dry the cheese and place in a ripening room, ripening box, or mini hothouse.

Info

After just 1 week, the cheese will taste slightly ripe. After 14 days, you can enjoy it, or, if you want a more mature cheese, leave it to ripen for longer. Keep a precise record of ripening times so you can refer to it next time you ripen cheese.

Semihard cheese with walnuts

MAKES APPROX.
7 OZ (200 G)

2 quarts (2 liters) full-
fat milk
2 tbsp (30 ml)
buttermilk (or
corresponding
amount of culture)
rennet (according to
the instructions on
the packet)
½ tsp (3 g) +
10 tbsp (200 g) salt
1 tbsp chopped
walnuts

▥ Place the milk in a pan and heat to 90 °F (32 °C) (use a thermometer). Stir in the buttermilk or culture, and leave to stand for 30 minutes. Add the rennet and water mixture, stir well. Bring the milk to a standstill with a counter movement of the whisk.

▥ Once the milk has formed a coagulum, cut it lengthwise and crosswise. Reheat the curds up to 104 °F (40 °C) while stirring constantly, then leave to stand for 30 minutes.

▥ Scoop the curds into prepared cheese molds, add the walnuts and ½ tsp (3 g) of salt, and let the whey drain away for 1 hour. Then turn the cheese and leave the whey to drain away again.

▥ Beginning with a weight of 2 pounds (1 kg), press for 1 hour, turn the cheese and press for another hour. Then press with 6½ pounds (3 kg) for 1 hour, turn the cheese, and press for another hour.

▥ Place the cheese in a 20% brine solution for 1 hour (see page 153). Dry the cheese on the outside and place in a ripening room or ripening box.

TIP

This walnut cheese tastes delicious served with crusty carrot bread.

Semihard cheese with herbs

MAKES APPROX.
7 OZ (200 G)

2 quarts (2 liters) full-
fat milk
2 tbsp (30 ml)
buttermilk (or
corresponding
amount of culture)
rennet (according to
the instructions on
the packet)
½ tsp herb salt
10 tbsp (200 g) salt

▓ Place the milk in a pan and heat to 93 °F (34 °C) (use a thermometer). Stir in the buttermilk or culture. Leave to stand for 30 minutes. Add the rennet and water mixture, stir well. Bring the milk to a standstill with a counter movement of the whisk.

▓ Once the milk has formed a coagulum, cut it lengthwise and crosswise. Reheat the curds to 107 °F (42 °C) while stirring constantly. The curds should be pea size. Leave to stand for 30 minutes.

▓ Scoop the curds into prepared cheese molds, mix with herb salt. Allow the whey to drain away for 1 hour, then turn the cheese and allow the whey to drain away for another hour.

▓ Beginning with a weight of 2 pounds (1 kg), press for 1 hour, turn the cheese and press for another hour. Then press with 6½ pounds (3 kg) for 1 hour, turn the cheese, and press for another hour.

▓ Place the cheese in a 20% brine solution for 1 hour (see page 153). Dry the cheese on the outside and place in a ripening room or ripening box.

VARIATIONS

For peperoncini cheese, add ½ teaspoon dried peperoncini and salt instead of herb salt.

A cheese for every dish

Every type of cheese has its own consistency and flavor. The intensity of the flavor will also differ. The type of cheese you use for individual dishes is a matter of personal preference. All the same, there are traditional combinations of cheese that go very well together—for example, pesto with Parmesan, and Kasnocken (Austrian cheese dumplings) with the original Räucherkäse (smoked cheese).

Use	Cheese type
Topping with melted cheese	Fresh soft cheese, Gouda, or Tilsiter
Vegetable strudel/salad	Feta
Cheese fondue	Emmentaler, Freiburger, Tilsiter, Appenzeller, Gruyère
Pasta/Pesto	Parmesan
Tomato/vegetable pizza	Mozzarella

A visit to a typical Bavarian local dairy

Traditional dairy farmers based in the Tegernsee region of the Bavarian Alps set up a cooperative in order to make their own cheese from their pasture milk. "Naturkäserei TegernseerLand eG" stands for high quality and a sustainable dairy industry. Their pretty building on the Wallberg mountain near Kreuth contains a restaurant serving traditional light meals, a cheese shop, and a working dairy, where you can watch the cheese being made and sample it on site.

A tour of the working dairy

The raw milk supplied by 20 family businesses is processed daily in the working dairy. You can watch the cheese-makers at work through its large window. The finished cheeses are stored in the cellar to ripen, where they are smeared by hand daily. The dairy workers offer guided tours of the building. In the herb garden, a herb expert is on hand to explain about the various spices and tea and medicinal herbs planted there. A few herb types are used to enhance the milk cheeses made from grass-fed cow's milk. In the dairy, consumers can learn a lot about the art of cheese-making and the grass-fed milk industry, with first-hand information offered. If you fancy a traditional Bavarian snack or a glass of fresh local milk, you can relax in the restaurant, or on the terrace with a view of the mountains. Choose from traditional Bavarian snacks and light lunches served with cheese. The adjacent shop sells all kinds of things made from the milk of grass-fed cows—cheeses, yogurts, and fresh milk—as well as fresh farmhouse bread, honey, Schnapps, and condiments.

Full-flavored—Tegernseer Bergkas (Tegernsee mountain cheese)

One example of the many flavorful pasture milk products made by Naturkäserei TegernseerLand eG is the medium-age Tegernseer Bergkas, a rustic hard cheese made from raw grass-fed cow's milk. The 33 pound (15 kg) cheeses are aged for at least six months and regularly "cared for"—that is, smeared by hand. During the ripening period, a reddish-brown and wholesome natural rind forms, with the help of red smear cultures. The mountain cheese has a few holes the size of cherry pits in it. The beneficial raw milk flora provide the characteristic, unmistakable flavor.

The differences between summer and winter cheese are interesting. Summer milk contains more unsaturated fatty acids and more of the natural pigment beta-carotene. This makes the cheese yellower and more elastic. Winter cheese is crumblier and more ivory in color. These features differentiate this handmade natural product.

Serve with a medium red wine or a robust, full-bodied white wine. Tegernseer Bergkas is also a very good cheese to use in cooking, for example in this quiche.

The master cheese-makers regularly check the taste and consistency of the cheese made from the milk of grass-fed cows. This includes looking after the rind by checking it and smearing it by hand.

Quiche with mountain cheese

For the pastry
generous 1⅓ cups
(200 g) flour
7 tbsp (100 g) butter
3½ tbsp (50 ml)
water
½ tsp salt
flour for the counter
fat and flour for the
pan

■ To make the pastry, knead all the ingredients together, wrap in plastic wrap, and chill for 30 minutes.

■ Preheat the oven to 350 °F (180 °C), grease the pan, and dust with flour. Then roll the pastry out on a floured counter and place in the springform pan, pressing the pastry down well and leaving a ¾ inch (2 cm) overhang. Pierce with a fork and prebake in the hot oven for 15 minutes, then remove from the oven and leave to cool.

■ Preheat the oven to 390 °F (200 °C). To make the filling, spread the ham, carrots, and green onions over the base. Whisk together the eggs, cream, and cheese and season with salt, pepper, and nutmeg. Pour the cream mixture over the ingredients and bake the quiche in the hot oven for 30 minutes. Serve with a fresh salad.

For the filling
1¼ cups (200 g)
cubed ham
3 carrots cut into
slices
3 green onions cut
into slices
3 eggs
generous ¾ cup
(200 ml) cream
1¾ cups (200 g)
grated cheese (e.g.
Tegernseer Bergkas,
Wallberger)
salt, pepper
freshly grated
nutmeg

At a glance

Basic equipment

Pans and crockery – you should use your own crockery for making dairy products. Pans without thermal bases are best, as thermal bases reheat the milk by up to 11 °F (6 °C). You should also buy a separate whisk and sieve that you only use for dairy processing.

Thermometer – the best kind is a 12 inch (30 cm) food thermometer, which you can buy from a specialist store.

Cultures – you can work with special starter cultures, however yogurt or buttermilk is also suitable for home use.

Rennet – is available in liquid form or as tablets or powder. Liquid rennet is best for small quantities, in my experience.

Cheesecloths and curd cloths – please buy specialist products for cheese-making. Household cloths sometimes work for whey drainage. However, if the fabric does not have the right structure, the whey will not drain properly.

Cheese molds – come in a variety of sizes. The softer the consistency of the curds, the finer the holes in the cheese molds should be. Two molds are usually enough to start with, until you become more familiar with dairy processing.

Cheese press – available from specialist cheese stores, and recommended even for small cheese quantities. To start with, however, it is fine to use alternatives. This could be sandblasting grains in sealed jars, or salt or flour in a plastic bag.

How to recognize and avoid defective products

Anyone who tries their hand at making dairy products will soon realize that knowledge alone is not enough. You might make a perfect product one day, and a defective product the next.

Whenever I run a dairy processing course, participants always recount their experiences of failed dairy products. I have put together a checklist below. However, the causes are so numerous that it is sometimes difficult to know why a product has failed. It is useful to keep a written record of the process, then you can usually work out what went wrong.

Defect cause checklist

Weather – cheese-makers always tell me that the milk turns sour more quickly if there is a storm approaching, as well as on hot summer days.

Feeding with silage – the composition of the milk changes if the animals are fed with silage. In my experience, cheese can occasionally succeed with milk from animals that are fed with silage, but a completely defective product may be the result (see page 24).

Yeast and other unwanted bacteria – if there are any unwanted bacteria on the equipment you use for dairy processing, it is not enough to wash it under hot water. These pieces of equipment must be boiled. Unwanted bacteria can also occur in liquid rennet if you leave the bottle open for too long.

Contaminated cultures – cultures are packaged very hygienically, so any defect is more likely to come from our usage. An example is when we have opened a package of cultures and not used them immediately.

Cloths and cheese molds – both are real breeding grounds for bacteria. You should therefore boil them after each use, making sure that the holes in the cheese molds are cleaned thoroughly.

Avoiding defective products is possible to a certain extent, provided you check each time you are making cheese that you have considered the factors above. Don't take risks. Throw any dairy product away immediately if it does not taste or smell as it should. With bought products, we tend to rely on the expiration date, and our sense of taste may therefore not be as acute as it used to be. Making your own dairy products is a good way to retune your taste buds so they can tell whether a foodstuff is really safe to eat. Industrially manufactured foods are subject to very strict regulatory controls. We should be just as strict with domestically produced food.

Quick recipes with step-by-step photos

Below are brief summaries of the individual steps for the three main homemade dairy product recipes, quark, yogurt, and fresh soft cheese. I have also provided step-by-step photos. These recipes correspond to the main recipes contained in the relevant chapters earlier in the book.

Quark

MAKES
2 ½–3 ½ CUPS
(800–900 G)

3 quarts (3 liters) milk
½ cup (125 ml) buttermilk
rennet (approx. ⅓ of the quantity for cheese according to the instructions on the packet)

▥ Heat the milk to 90 °F (32 °C).

▥ Add the buttermilk and stir well. Leave the inoculated milk to stand in a warm place for about 30 minutes.

▥ Thin the rennet with water and add to the inoculated milk. Leave to stand in a warm place for about 24 hours. There should be a greenish whey on the top and the quark should come away from the edge and stick together.

▥ Cut the coagulum lengthwise and crosswise. Leave for 1 hour.

▥ Scoop the quark into a curd cloth, hang the curd cloth up, and move it back and forth from time to time. Using a spatula, scrape the dry quark from the edges of the cloth—this guarantees optimal whey drainage. As soon as the quark is ready, place it in an airtight container.
(See page 92 for the main recipe.)

Yogurt

▦ Heat the milk to 107 °F (42 °C) (or, if you are using a culture, to the temperature stated in the instructions).

▦ Add the yogurt or the culture, stir well.

▦ Pour the mixture into prepared jars (or yogurt containers). Leave to incubate for a few hours in the yogurt maker.
(See page 38 for the main recipe.)

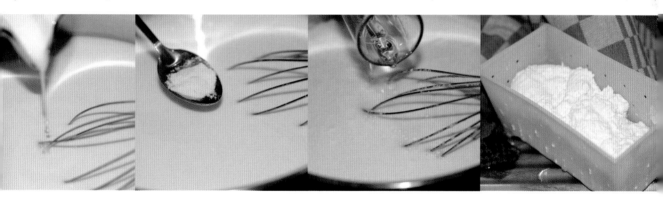

Fresh soft cheese

▦ Heat the milk to 95 °F (36 °C).

▦ Stir in the buttermilk or culture.

▦ Stir in the rennet that has been thinned with water.

▦ Once the milk has formed a coagulum, cut it lengthwise and crosswise. Leave to stand for 30 minutes, then carefully scoop into the prepared cheese molds.
(See page 124 for the main recipe.)

Indexes

Subject index

Recipe index

Note: The oven temperatures in this book are given for ovens with top and bottom heat. When using a convection oven, please adjust the temperatures according to the manufacturer's instructions.

Author acknowledgments

A few lines to end with ...

The world of dairy products is inexhaustible. As a child, I knew by heart the path to the farm where we fetched our daily milk. My first book about dairy products, written many years ago, combined my love of writing, cooking, experimenting, and photography. At the time I had very simple resources, five small children in the kitchen as helpers, and plenty of work on the farm. I have carried with me the desire to pass on my collected experiences to other people and to inspire people to make their own dairy products.

The work on this new book, which you hold in your hands, brought back many memories for me. I hope you can feel the love and joy I have put into this book, from the preparations, to writing the recipes and procedures, to photographing the delicious dairy products.

I am very grateful to Kathrin Gritschneder, a wonderful editor. She edited my manuscript consistently. Lots of pages went back and forth between St. Johann and Deggendorf! I have her to thank that this book, alongside my practical knowledge, also contains so much expertise on the subject of nutrition. Thank you, Kathrin!

Christine Pazmann designed a unique layout, for which I am very grateful—the perfect way to showcase the world of dairy products.

Dear Hermann, Sandra, Herm, Chri, Manuel, and Stefanie, thank you for your support, which I can always rely on! And I thank God for His love and power, which I continue to experience through Him.

Publisher acknowledgments

Special thanks go to the following companies for their contributions to the book:

Landesvereinigung der Bayerischen Milchwirtschaft e.V.
Josef Stemmer
Kaiser-Ludwig-Platz 2
80336 München
www.milchland-bayern.de

Naturkäserei TegernseerLand eG
Florian Hauder
Reißenbichlweg 1
83708 Kreuth
www.naturkaeserei.de

Tourismusverband Großarltal
Dir. Thomas Wirnsperger
Markt 1
A-5611 Großarl
www.grossarltal.info

Picture credits

Erhardt, Matthias: pp. 158 both, 159

Flegel, Cordula: pp. 24 all, 25

Fotolia: outside front cover, outside back cover small left, pp. 4 bottom, 14 small left, 15, 20, 22, 31, 33, 35, 82 small middle, 82 small right, 90, 92 both, 94 left, 96 right, 97, 106, 107, 123, 134 both, 135 both bottom

Huber, Heidi: outside back cover small right, pp. 28, 30 small middle, 30 small right, 38 right, 40 both, 41, 42 both, 43 both, 44, 45, 46 both, 51, 53 both, 54, 57, 59, 60, 61, 64, 65, 68, 72, 77, 79, 80, 82 large, 93 both, 94 right, 95, 96 left, 98, 102, 104, 109, 112, 113, 114, 115, 116 all, 121, 122, 124, 125, 127, 130, 131, 136 both, 137, 139, 155, 162 all, 163 all

iStockphoto: outside back cover small middle, p.p 4 top, 14 small middle, 14 small right, 19 left, 26, 32

Landesvereinigung der Bayerischen Milchwirtschaft LVBM: p. 150

Bildagentur Look: pp. 13, 21, 29, 67

Stockfood: pp. 5 both, 6 both, 7, 8 all, 9, 14 large, 16 both, 17, 19 right, 23, 30 large, 30 small left, 38 left, 39, 48 both, 49, 55, 62 all, 63, 71 both, 74 both, 75 both, 82 small left, 85, 86, 87, 89, 91, 99, 108, 110, 111, 118 both, 129, 132 both, 133, 135 both top, 140 all, 143, 145, 149, 151, 153, 157

SZ-Photo: p.p 10 (SSPL), 11 (Scherl)

Ullstein Bild: p. 12 top (Herbert Hoffmann), bottom (imagebroker.net/Bahnmüller)

www.großarltal.info: pp. 100 both, 101

Disclaimer

The information and recipes printed in this book are provided to the best of our knowledge and belief and from our own experience. However neither the author nor the publisher shall accept liability for any damage whatsoever which may arise directly or indirectly from the use of this book. This disclaimer applies in particular to the use and consumption of untreated raw milk and/or raw milk products, which the author and publisher strongly advise against due to the associated health risks.

It is advisable not to serve dishes that contain raw eggs to very young children, pregnant women, elderly people, or to anyone weakened by serious illness. If in any doubt, consult your doctor. Be sure that all the eggs you use are as fresh as possible.

© Verlags- und Vertriebsgesellschaft Dort- Hagenhausen Verlag- GmbH & Co. KG, Munich

Original Title: *Alles von der Milch. Köstlich & selbst gemacht*

ISBN 978-3-86362-013-4

Editing and assistance with product information: Kathrin Gritschneder

Layout and design: Christine Paxmann text · konzept · grafik, Munich

© for this English edition: h.f.ullmann publishing GmbH

Translation from German: Rebekah Wilson in association with First Edition Translations Ltd, Cambridge, UK

Editing: Jenny Knight in association with First Edition Translations Ltd, Cambridge, UK

Typesetting: The Write Idea in association with First Edition Translations Ltd, Cambridge, UK

Project management for h.f.ullmann publishing: Katharina Pferdmenges, Isabel Weiler

Overall responsibility for production: h.f.ullmann publishing GmbH, Potsdam, Germany

Printed in India, 2015

ISBN 978-3-8480-0805-6

10 9 8 7 6 5 4 3 2 1
X IX VIII VII VI V IV III II I

www.ullmann-publishing.com
newsletter@ullmann-publishing.com
facebook.com/ullmann.social